EDUCATOR REFLECTION TIPS VOLUME II

Refining Our Practice

Jami Fowler-White

ConnectEDD Publishing
Chicago, Illinois

This publication is available at discount pricing when purchased in quantity for educational purposes, promotions, or fundraisers. For inquiries and details, contact the publisher at:

info@connecteddpublishing.com

Published by ConnectEDD Publishing LLC
Chicago, IL
www.connecteddpublishing.com

Cover Design: Kheila Dunkerly

Educator Reflection Tips Volume II: Refining Our Practice/ Jami Fowler-White.
—1st ed.

Paperback ISBN: 978-1-7348908-8-4

Praise for *Educator Reflection Tips, Volume II*

Reflecting on our experiences allows us to grow from them. But how can we reflect and on what should we reflect? This guide provides you the tools necessary to become a reflective practitioner and increase the impact you have on students' learning. And, it will help you feel even better about yourself as you realize the skills you are developing.

—**Douglas Fisher,** Author, San Diego State University

Educator Reflection Tips Vol. 2 is a book I needed as a teacher. Jami Fowler-White has compiled the questions that educators are asking themselves and each other on a daily basis, yet don't always have the time to delve deeply into during planning periods. But what if they did? What if teachers looked at these reflection questions, chose one to read and reflect on before planning their next lessons and units, and then entered the planning, teaching and reflection cycle better equipped and set up for success? This book guides educators through the reflection process with research-based explanations, practical strategies, and additional resources to deepen learning right at our fingertips. The answers to these questions are within us as educators and Jami leads us to finding them in a most engaging, non-judgmental voice that we all need to hear.

— **Trelane Clark,** M.A.T., C.A.G.S.

Do you want to have high student achievement and engagement? Jami Fowler-White guides you to stop, think, reflect, and transform. She pushes your thinking to go beyond the status quo for *all* students. She doesn't just tell you to reflect and transform but provides simple, doable steps and strategies rooted in research.

— **Pamela Hall,** Award-winning Educator,
   Author, & Speaker at pamhall2inspire.com

Jami takes educators on a journey towards the realization that self-reflection is key in improving their instructional practice. The *Educator Reflection Tips* series is an essential tool for all educators. Its unique format make it the perfect tool for school leaders to use in Professional

Learning Communities, Book Studies, as well as when mentoring new/ novice teachers. I highly recommend this volume, especially as it will help educators think through effective methods to engage students, integrate technology, and navigate the day-to-day changes of teaching and learning.

— **Kongsouly Sengchannovong Jones,** Assistant
Superintendent of Schools, Shelby County Schools (TN)

What separates a good teacher from a great teacher is the ability to reflect. At the top of Bloom's Taxonomy is Creation, but when we can take the time to reflect on what we have created then spend the time to make it better, we have really entered into a world of excellence. In this book, Jami guides us through a reflective journey, not just by telling us what we need to create, but by asking us what we need to improve. I am so grateful that Jami was willing to put this book into the world to allow us all to continue to grow, inspire, and improve."

— **Dr. Dave Schmittou,** Author, Speaker,
Educational Change Agent

Fowler-White, shares a powerful and in-depth work offering a plethora of relevant, refreshing, and insightful strategies and resources. Her unique approach to educator practice aligns with various perspectives from inquiry, guidance, and activities to deeply enrich the experience of reflection within a variety of platforms. Fowler-White strategically explores the implementation of reflection, empowering stakeholders beyond educators including families with respect to cultural relevance. As Fowler White's inquisitive take on a "deeper dive into the core reflective inquiry" the unique treasures hidden within this book will profoundly impact teaching and learning for all who are engaged in any learning environment.

— **Dr. Dolores Cormier-Zenon,** NBCT; *Vice-Chairman,*
National Board Network of Minoritized Educators

Dedication

To my family...

I am most grateful to my husband, Fred, my son, DeVon, my other, Lydia, and my sister, Felicia, for their sacrifices and unwavering support over the last six months as I have worked to create the first two volumes of the *Educator Reflection Tips* series. There are no words to express my thanks for the late nights, missed meals, free editing services, advice, and encouragement. I appreciate each of you more than you know.

EDUCATOR REFLECTION TIPS VOLUME II

Refining Our Practice

Jami Fowler-White

Table of Contents

EDUCATOR REFLECTION TIPS VOLUME II

Introduction

Imagine earning your bachelor's degree in Elementary Education in December and spending months working as a substitute teacher due to the lack of job openings in the surrounding school districts. If you've never had the luxury of serving as a substitute teacher, I'm here to tell you that it is nothing like having your own classroom. I often wonder had I known what was ahead, would I have chosen to spend more time in other grade levels honing my craft. In February, I accepted a nine-week position as a Kindergarten substitute for a teacher on maternity leave. Six weeks later, I had just put the students down for an afternoon nap when Mrs. Whitney, the principal, came into the classroom and offered me a full-time teaching position.

The myriad of emotions I experienced in that moment were indescribable. However, I did not have time to bask in the joy of landing my first job for long. You see, one of the second-grade teachers abruptly resigned and I only had the weekend to prepare and make the space my own. My family and I spent ALL weekend making my first classroom look and feel warm and inviting. I consider the classroom to be a student's second home. After all, students spend eight hours each day in that room and it should be a comfortable place for them.

Next to parents, teachers are the most constant person in a student's life. I wanted everything to be perfect for those twenty second graders who I was blessed to have in my classroom. When you are seven, you do not understand why your teacher leaves on a Friday and never returns and I wanted to do everything in my power to help the students understand. There was a lot of time spent that first week helping students cope with the change while building relationships with them. Then the unthinkable happened—on Day 10 (again this was a Friday), Human Resources assigned me to a new school, and I had to report the following Monday. I was crushed, disappointed, and utterly devastated, questioning why this was happening to me. It broke my heart to tell my students that I would not be able to continue as their teacher. In a span of two weeks, these students had lost two teachers. To make a long story short, the district's policy prohibited relatives from working together if it was their first job. My sister was a third-grade teacher at the school and since this was my first teaching position, I had to transfer and finish the year at a different school.

My second "first" teaching job: For the second time in two weeks, I walked into a classroom that needed to be transformed into a cozy and welcoming space for students over another weekend. Monday, I met my second set of second grade students as teacher NUMBER FIVE in their second grade experience.

Remember this was February and the school year ended in June. Can you imagine having four teachers leave and never come back in a single school year? Admittedly, this was the hardest year that I have ever had as a teacher. Children deserve a stable learning environment, one in which they trust their teacher, know he/she cares, understands them, and is invested in helping them to grow and excel. When I stood in front of this new set of students, I could see the fear, distrust, and hopelessness on their faces. They had been robbed of the joy of being a second grader.

Social and emotional well-being is vital for optimal learning to occur. Every student should feel safe and be able to trust their teachers. It is imperative educators are intentional about the environment cultivated within their classrooms, no matter the setting. It took a great deal of patience and understanding, but I was finally able to restore my students' trust in the education system by consistently showing them I cared and supporting them.

This experience was a type of unspoken trauma that no student should be subjected to. I do not know why the teachers before me chose to leave the school. Reflecting on this time in my career, I am grateful for the experience, despite the daunting challenges I faced. The time spent rebuilding their trust and restoring their love for school proved how resilient children are when given adequate support. I cannot say each student was fully prepared academically when they entered third grade, but I can wholeheartedly attest to the fact that they were socially and emotionally well and eager to learn. Research shows that a single traumatic event can have a long-term adverse impact on students' academic growth and progress (Abdelnoor & Hollins, 2004; Gibbs et al., 2019, Weems et al., 2013). Thanks to my training on Maslow's hierarchy of needs, I was able to utilize my toolkit of non-clinical social and emotional strategies to restore students' trust in teachers and the educational system.

The Premise of Educator Reflection Tips

Educators, especially teachers, spend nearly every moment of the day thinking about future lessons, reflecting on past lessons, and wondering what more they can do to ensure that their students are successful—both academically and in life. With this in mind, in December 2019, I began offering bite-size professional learning opportunities on Twitter through the lens of reflective questions to remind educators about the importance of growing professionally.

Within six months, I realized that I needed more than 280 characters to thoroughly explain a topic and help educators improve their practice. *DigitialPD4You*™, a professional development company which provides professional development, educational tools, and resources for school leaders and teachers, was born amid the Coronavirus pandemic after I published the first *50 Educator Reflection Tips* on Twitter. This allowed me the opportunity to support the development of other educators by providing reflective questions on all aspects of teaching and learning, sharing research-based quick tips, and linking additional articles, books, and online resources for teachers and school leaders to learn more on each topic. My first book, *Educator Reflection Tips Volume #1* was published as a deeper dive into the reflection tips I had offered online. Each chapter includes an activity to facilitate the development of a tangible plan or product to use in the classroom, an infographic for educators as a reminder about the knowledge gained, as well as a chart of additional resources to help educators continue to learn and grow.

The *Educator Reflection Tips* series is unique in that each chapter spotlights specific issues facing educators, offering a research-based focus for improving practice in each area. This distinctive feature enables teachers to strengthen their knowledge of instructional practices in multiple areas using one source.

Educator Reflection Tips, Volume II is organized into four distinct clusters:

1. *Classroom Competencies* outlines instructional strategies educators can incorporate into their practice.
2. *Critical Literacy* provides guidance on teaching students to learn to read and read to learn.
3. *Cyber Connection* contains strategies to help students become digitally literate.
4. *Classroom Culture* provides guidelines for developing relationships and meeting the diverse needs of students.

Each topic in this book is written succinctly and independent of the other chapters. Although the topics have been grouped into competencies, *Educator Reflection Tips* is not a book that requires you to read the chapters in order. Each Reflection Tip should be thought of as an individual, bite-size professional development session. Go back to the Table of Contents and review the reflection tip premise for each

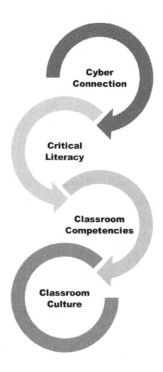

chapter. Rank them based on what you believe will have the most impact on your practice from one (most significant) to ten (least significant). Record the numbers (#) of your first five tips below. Consider reading the corresponding chapters first, since they are likely to have the most immediate impact on student outcomes and your instructional practice. While reading the selected tips, take notes and create a plan describing your action steps for implementation. Thank you for choosing to serve as an educator and for always striving to improve your practice!

My Top Five Reflection Tips

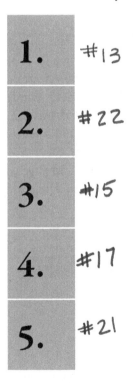

1.   #13

2.   #22

3.   #15

4.   #17

5.   #21

The Case for Self-Reflection

*"Self-reflection entails asking yourself questions about your values,
assessing your strengths and failures, thinking about your perceptions
and interactions with others, and imagining where
you want to take your life in the future."*

Robert L. Rosen

What is Self-Reflection?

Reflection involves internalizing all aspects of your practice. This includes examining the good, the bad, the ugly—and then determining what you have learned from each experience. If you look up the definition of self-reflection, Merriam-Webster defines it as "careful thought about your own beliefs and behaviors" (Self-reflection, n.d.). Upon reading this definition, I found myself wondering exactly what "careful thought" looks and sounds like for an educator. In essence, careful thought is thinking about one's actions, behaviors, and beliefs and using these experiences to strengthen classroom practices. Of course, developing self-reflection skills is not a simple process. Hall and Simeral (2008) share a continuum (see chart below) of self-reflection to explore on our journey to honing our instructional craft:

Adapted from Self-Reflection Continuum: Hall & Simeral 2008

According to Hall and Simeral (2008), self-reflection follows a continuum comprised of the following stages:

1. **Unaware:** In this stage, educators are not cognizant of the inconsistencies within their practice. Teachers in this stage

exhibit a focus on routines, collaboration on a superficial level, inaccurate descriptions of problems of practice, scripted instruction with little to no differentiation or evidence of systematic, standards-driven planning. Additionally, educators struggle with time management and helping students make connections with the curriculum. The focus for educators in this stage is to build self-awareness.

2. **Conscious:** Practitioners in this stage exhibit a consistent gap between knowing what should be done and executing these actions, make excuses for problems, become easily sidetracked from meeting anticipated goals, collaborate inconsistently within the work environment, dismiss other colleagues' beliefs, implement lessons using strategies that are teacher-focused, make occasional links between teaching and learning, sometimes differentiate, and inconsistently plan for instruction. When educators are in this stage, the focus should be on planning and strengthening pedagogical knowledge.

3. **Action:** Teachers who are at this level of self-reflection habitually use data from assessments to examine student progress, view student success as a measure of their own success, collaborate on a limited basis, incorporate research-based practices, plan standards-driven instruction, believe there is only one path to success, and reflect daily but struggle with long-term problem solving. To help educators move beyond this stage, the focus should be on helping to strengthen teachers' expertise and help them to use the knowledge to make instructional decisions.

4. **Refinement:** Educators in this final stage reflect continuously throughout the school day, understand there is more than one route to success, use assessment to drive instruction, build student ownership in the learning process, plan lessons based on students' academic needs, seek out opportunities to learn and grow with peers, and continuously work to add strategies to their instructional toolbox. Ultimately, this is the stage all educators should seek to attain. Once this level is reached, the focus should be on creating a plan for continuous reflection and long-term growth (Hall and Simeral, 2008, p. 40-44).

STOP & REFLECT

After reading about the self-reflection continuum, stop and answer the following questions:

1. **Seeking Refinement**: How often do you think about your level of expertise in the classroom?

2. **Self-Reflection Rating**: Where would you place yourself within the self-reflection continuum?

3. **Reality Check**: Am I currently using self-reflection? If not, what is hindering me from using the reflection process?

4. **Impact of Feedback**: How receptive are you to feedback from administrators, your peers, your students, or parents?

5. **Data-Driven Instruction**: What method are you currently using to track students' growth and progress?

Why Should I Practice Self-Reflection?

According to Richard Henry Dunn, "He who dares to teach must never cease to learn" (Fiore & Whitaker, 2005, p.148). I used to think I was doing a great job of reflecting on my practice. In my work as an Instructional Coach, I spent a lot of time helping teachers learn about the power of self-reflection, but after being in the field for over two decades I will admit that pre-COVID-19, I was working on autopilot.

One silver lining from the pandemic has been the gift of time—time to sit still and truly reflect on my practice. As educators continue to navigate through the unpredictability of the pandemic and its effect on the educational system, self-reflection is a must. Navigating through changes requires teachers to continuously reflect and recalibrate their skills as they reimagine teaching and learning. It is also crucial to remember that regardless of whether you are new to teaching or have been in the profession several years, your level of self-reflection matters. According to Hall and Simeral (2008), a teacher's capacity to self-reflect on their practice is directly correlated to their level of effectiveness within the profession (p. 38). Since no educator sets out to be unsuccessful at their craft, the first reflection tip in this volume is dedicated to helping create a reflective mindset. Mindset is simply one's mental attitude. More time will be spent discussing the topic of mindset in Reflection Tip #13. If you are not familiar with Dr. Carol Dweck's research on mindset, this chapter will help you continue moving towards self-reflection.

Transformational Reflection and Habits of Effectiveness

Now that the stages of self-reflection have been identified, let's examine how to transform teaching and learning inside your classroom by implementing self-reflection. Black and Plowright (2010) regard reflection as a multidimensional process of using knowledge and instructional training in combination with critically examining and assessing that learning or practice. The aim of reflection is to advance an educator's specialized knowledge, understanding, and training to includeThe aim of reflection is to advance specialized knowledge, understanding, and training that encompasses a greater system of learning which is "transformational in nature and empowering, enlightening, and ultimately emancipatory" (p. 247).

Each stage of this multidimensional model of self-reflection is outlined below.

Believing in yourself and your students while seeking to form a habit of effectiveness is essential as you progress on the journey to transformational self-reflection (Canter et al, 1994). Note that this is a cyclical process that once formed into a habit, will become a routine. The pillars of the habit of effectiveness include using data to focus your work, creating a goal to work towards, and intentionally integrating practices that will move students closer to attaining mastery of standards. When you first begin to work through this cycle, seek the support of administrators, a mentor, or a school or district level coach to help you monitor progress at each stage. Educators who are in the process of learning to self-reflect benefit from the guidance and feedback of coaches, mentors, and school

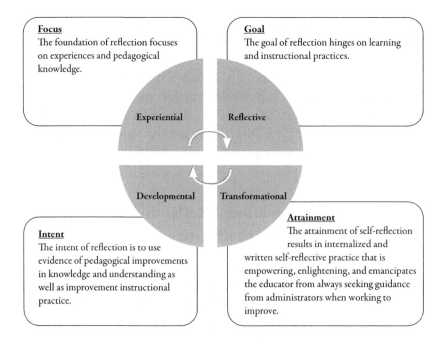

Focus
The foundation of reflection focuses on experiences and pedagogical knowledge.

Goal
The goal of reflection hinges on learning and instructional practices.

Experiential

Reflective

Developmental

Transformational

Intent
The intent of reflection is to use evidence of pedagogical improvements in knowledge and understanding as well as improvement instructional practice.

Attainment
The attainment of self-reflection results in internalized and written self-reflective practice that is empowering, enlightening, and emancipates the educator from always seeking guidance from administrators when working to improve.

Adapted from Black and Plowright, 2010, p. 248-251

leaders who have observed their practice. A more in-depth discussion of this topic will be examined in Volume #3 of the *Educator Reflection Tip* series. It will discuss the value of continuing to grow yourself and others. As you resume this repetitive cycle, your goal should be to move with automaticity through each stage, monitoring and adjusting your own progress without the assistance of other people.

Whether you believe it or not, *you* are the most important factor in a child's academic success. The intent of this chapter is not to make you doubt your ability. The purpose is to equip you with the knowledge you need to attain transformational reflection, so you have the most profound impact on student outcomes. The choices you make instructionally each day shape not only your destiny, but every student within your care.

STOP & REFLECT

Identify where you think you are within Black and Plowright's Multidimensional attainment of Transformational reflection:

Why did you give yourself this rating? What evidence supports the level that you chose?

Pedagogical Preparation: What is your plan to improve your content knowledge and instructional toolkit?

Accountability Preference: How will you work toward the transformational level of self-reflection? Do you prefer to begin to keep a daily/weekly journal, develop a method to track student progress, or have an accountability partner?

What's Next?

Each volume of *Educator Reflection Tips* is intended to build upon the other. Therefore, instead of beginning with #1 as customarily done by most authors, I have chosen to begin this volume as a continuation and number the first Reflection Tip of this volume #13, picking up where we left off in Volume I. As I contemplated over whether I should begin this second volume with #1, I thought it would be easier for readers, to compartmentalize and catalog their knowledge if each tip had its own unique number instead of having multiple tips with the same number. Although you are welcome to read each tip in the order written, I encourage you to start with the competency which will likely have the most impact on your instructional practice:

    #1-Classroom Competence
    #2-Critical Literacy
    #3-Cyber Connection or
    #4-Classroom Culture

Thank you for taking time to continue learning, reflecting, and growing yourself professionally. I'm excited about the journey that we are embarking on together. I think you are ready. Let's reflect together...

Part I

Classroom Competencies

"No matter how many mistakes you make or how slow your progress, you are still way ahead of everyone who is not trying."
Tony Robbins

Reflection Tip #13: Do you believe that mindset matters in the classroom?

As defined in Chapter 1, mindset is characterized as mental attitude. As we begin to wind down a school year unlike any other, it will be important for educators to make sure we have prepared ourselves mentally. We must provide daily support to students regarding the trauma they may have endured over the past few months and prepare for the challenges we will certainly face as the year progresses. Coronavirus Pandemic 2020 has been quite the year. This school year students have been changed in more ways than we can predict. There is no way to predict the issues we will encounter over the next few years. Therefore, students' mental welfare should be a priority.

What is Mindset?

Researchers have detected two categories of mindset. Dr. Carol Dweck is considered an expert on the idea of mindset. In her book, aptly titled, *Mindset: The New Psychology of Success*, she sheds light on mindset, and its impact on people in all aspects of life. The book begins with the definitions and attributes of the two mindsets. The first is a fixed mindset. A fixed mindset is based on the principle that achievement is the declaration of a person's innate intelligence, character, artistic, and creative skills. The other type of mindset has been coined as growth mindset. When you have a growth mindset, you welcome challenges and view failure not as an indication of lack of intelligence, but as a supportive mechanism for development and expanding existing capabilities. Research shows that intelligence can be nurtured, and that with a growth mindset, people can resolve to understand brand-new things and believe they can achieve (Dweck, 2008).

Characteristics of Mindset

Fixed Mindset	Growth Mindset
<ul><li>seeing effort as unproductive</li><li>ignoring feedback because it is seen as condemnation</li><li>avoiding challenges</li><li>being intimidated by the success of others</li></ul>	<ul><li>learning from constructive criticism</li><li>seeing effort as a pathway to mastery</li><li>enduring when facing hurdles</li><li>embracing challenges</li><li>finding value and motivation in the success stories of others</li></ul>

Dweck, 2008, pp. 6-7

Everyone suffers from a fixed mindset every now and then; the key is learning how to change your mindset because remaining in a fixed mindset frequently leads to plateauing early in life and failing to reach your full potential. Educators must believe that all students can accomplish great things. Therefore, it is vital for us to help students figure out their fixed mindset triggers so they can understand how to acknowledge them and begin to move ahead, learning and developing their full capabilities.

Confronting Your Fixed Mindset Triggers

Before discussing how to help students work towards having a growth mindset, think about your mindset thus far in your role as a professional educator.

> *"Genius is 1% motivation and 99% hard work"*
> ~Thomas Edison

Do you agree or disagree with Edison's statement? In terms of your own mindset, is this one of the pillars that you believe in? In 2016, *Education Week Research* found that only forty-five percent of K-12 educators were knowledgeable about the concept of a growth mindset. Of those that knew about the research surrounding mindset, nearly all believed that, when fostered, it could positively impact student achievement (Ahmed & Rosen, 2019). It is important to share Dweck's research with colleagues, parents, and students. A change in mindset could be the missing element to improving student achievement in your classroom. In any case, before teaching students to adopt a growth mindset, it will be important for you to be honest about the type of mindset you have, as well as whether you have been modeling a fixed or growth mindset for students.

STOP & REFLECT

To help you reflect further on your own mindset and identify your fixed mindset triggers, consider the following to see how you measure up. Directions: Provide a Yes or No response to answer each of the mindset statements written below:

1. I seek out opportunities to learn. **Y**
2. When I receive feedback from administrators, colleagues, parents, and students I deem it as constructive criticism. **Y**
3. I am not afraid to take risks and persevere when confronted with obstacles. **y**
4. I allow students to productively struggle instead of instantly rescuing them when they get stuck. **sort of**
5. I believe that students should be given the opportunity to self-correct assignments and assessments to recover lost points. **Y**

If you answered yes to all areas, skip to the next section; you are ready to move on and begin teaching this philosophy to students. If you answered no, to any of the questions, reflect and work to confront the fixed mindset triggers identified. These triggers are preventing you from fully embracing the growth mindset philosophy.

What is your plan to work on any fixed mindset triggers that were identified?

_____

_____

_____

_____

Helping Students Identify Fixed Mindset Triggers

To help students pinpoint their fixed mindset triggers, perform a simple task by having students answer these questions:

- How do you behave in response to receiving a grade on an assessment or classwork?
- What is your primary reaction when you fail to achieve a goal that you have established for yourself?
- Have you ever given up on an assignment, task, or test because you thought it was too difficult? In hindsight, what could you have done differently?

Tell students to review their answers. Ask if their responses state they get upset and stop working or if they keep trying and say to themselves, "I will do better next time." Then discuss the two mindsets using the "right now" and "moving forward" approach with students. The "right now" is a fixed mindset and focuses only on what is occurring now. The desired outcome is to have students begin to say, "Moving forward" when they do not accomplish a goal on the first try or when they do not achieve the grade they were shooting for on a test or assignment. "Moving forward" is an immensely powerful context for promoting growth. It teaches students to look forward to the future and remember that there is still time to work towards reaching a goal. Success takes time, so we want to make sure students understand that, by changing our words, we also change our mindset.

Ultimately, the goal within the classroom is to teach students to believe they can get smarter, effort makes them stronger, to expect to productively struggle as they persevere through assignments, and that they learn from mistakes.

Educators should teach students to modify their words:

Instead of	Say....
I do not know how to do it.	What am I missing?
I made a mistake.	Mistakes support my improvement.
It is good enough.	Is this really my best work?
I give up; I quit.	I can do this!

I cannot make this assignment any better.	I can always get better.
I am not good at this subject.	I am on the right track.

MakersEmpire.com suggests subsequent questions to use with students to support altering their mindset. Consider integrating them into your classroom feedback loop:

- *Did something go wrong?* Amazing! How can you use this mistake to improve your work?
- *Finished?* Really? Have you put in the work to accomplish a product you are proud of?
- *Stuck?* Great! What can you aim for next? What other approaches might there be?
- *Not pleased with your project?* Wonderful! Who can you ask for feedback from to make your project better?
- *Easy?* Right! How can we make this more difficult for you?
- *Pleased with your layout?* Congratulations! Where to next? What are your targets? (Dimitriadis, 2015)

STOP & REFLECT

Have you thought about the practices you will integrate daily to help ensure that students are mentally prepared for learning and striving for excellence? How effective were previous practices you have implemented to ensure this? What evidence do you have to support your response?

ADDITIONAL RESOURCES

Dr. Carol Dweck (TED Talk):

Putting Mindset Into Practice:

Parent Views On Mindset:

Mindset by Carol Dweck:

Infographics for each Reflection Tip are available for download at www.
DigitalPD4You.com

Reflection Tip #14: Are you meeting the needs of all levels of learners within the online learning environment?

"In education, technology can be a life-changer, a game changer, for kids who are both in school and out of school."

Queen Rania of Jordan

While technology has become a fundamental part of life, applicable and appurtenant usage still needs to be augmented in education. As more schools move to online instruction, it will be important to develop a system to measure student readiness and how learner perception influences academic achievement in an online environment. Online instruction is characterized as any type of teaching and learning which occurs using the World Wide Web (Lim, Morris, & Kupritz, 2007). Online instruction evolved from distance learning. Distance learning has progressed over four phases: printed teaching and learning materials, initial applications in computer wireless systems, online instruction, and web-based telecommunications. As schools continue to implement the practices of e-learning, inspecting and expanding the dimensions of students' readiness to learn in such a way have become increasingly significant. Doing this will assist teachers in planning better online educational experiences for students.

Researchers have attempted to identify the online qualities which influence student readiness and learner perception within the online environment. Here are a few such characteristics:

- Peng, Tai, & Wu (2006) declared that students' literacy in the area of using technology and knowledge of the Internet shapes their performance during online learning.

- Correspondingly, student proficiency in using the World Wide Web shapes their viewpoint and online actions (Tsai & Lin, 2004).
- Hung, Chou, Chen, and Own (2010) created the Online Learning Readiness Scale (OLRS), which is a multidimensional instrument to measure students' readiness for online learning. The researchers validated five features: "self-directed learning, motivation for learning, computer, Internet self-efficacy, learner control, and online communication self-efficacy" (p. 1080).
- Martin, Sun, Westine (2020) suggest that educators plan online academic experiences based on specific learner characteristics. These learner characteristics can be largely categorized as demographic features, intellectual features, mental characteristics, emotive, self-regulation, and qualities that serve as catalysts for motivation.
- Research has indicated that a variety of attributes contribute to students thriving within the online academic environment. Among these attributes are learner personality, introspection-extrospection, cognitive styles, critical thinking disposition, special needs, sensing and thinking, knowledge, academic performance, and motivation (Ilie & Cocorado, 2014).

In addition to student readiness, educators should pay close attention to the shortcomings that research has pinpointed regarding how learners perceive online instruction. One shortcoming is its narrow potential to engage students in learning experiences except in instances when the learners possess strong executive functioning skills, are experientially involved in the learning process, and are self-directed (Lim, Morris, & Kurpritz, 2007). Moreover, students also reported a lack of belonging or community during online learning, inhibiting the growth of shared feelings and sentiments between them, their peers, and the teacher. This lack of community prevented them from actively participating and flourishing in the online environment. The authors argue that these characteristics are some of the most significant aspects affecting student fulfillment and learning transfer efficiency. We will examine areas for educators to consider when planning online experiences for students.

STOP & REFLECT

Reflect on the following questions:

1. Which of the student readiness characteristics on page 32 most resonated with you? Why?
2. Are there qualities of your personality which may negatively impact or influence how you plan and implement instruction? How will you begin working to reverse this impact?
3. How could using personality questionnaires with students positively impact your instructional practice?
4. Which personality traits do you believe are the most important to consider when planning online experiences for students? Why do you think these are the most important?

Learner Personality

There has always been a need for teachers to get to know their students academically, socially, and emotionally. This involves educators observing students as they interact with their peers, as they interact within the academic setting, and when possible the world outside of school. The sudden shift to online learning around the world due to the Coronavirus pandemic has caused educators to shift the methods traditionally used to discover the personality of each individual student. Despite the impermanence (one hopes) regarding this change, the use of technology in the academic environment will likely continue to escalate, including online learning options. Therefore, teachers will need to establish mechanisms for connecting with, relating to, and personalizing online instructional experiences. Personality is something that everybody knows exists, but nobody really understands how to define it (Scheewind & Rupert, 1998). Though difficult, in order to prepare lessons which meet the needs of all learners, teachers need to understand certain aspects of students personalities. For example, do you think knowing whether students identified as introverts or extraverts could be useful when planning online learning experiences? Let's analyze the qualities of both before determining the implications for the online environment.

Introverts

Better expressive when writing than during conversation.
Enjoy time spent alone in solitude.
Prefer one-on-one conversations or small groups
Dislike speaking on the telephone
Need time to think before speaking

Extroverts

Good conversationalists, active, and lively
Habitually outgoing, venture with confidence into unknown situations
Prefer outdoor activities, tend to be very sociable
Good leaders of big and small groups
Adapt easily and are happiest in social situations.

Photo Credit: istockphoto.com; Skynesher.com

Research (Downing, 2010) has yielded some interesting findings related to introverts and extroverts, indicating that introverts tend to thrive in the online learning environment due to the absence of the social interactions found within brick-and-mortar learning. Some introverted students prefer the online asynchronous communication method because it provides them more time to be reflective. They would rather learn and contribute during online discussions while many extroverts prefer attending school face-to-face. If the face-to-face option is not available, teachers have found that extroverts tend to connect better when their tasks include threaded communications because they are able to interact with multiple peers simultaneously.

Learner Independence

Several web-based instructional researchers have found student independence as a crucial element in academic achievement (Holmberg, 1995; Jung, 2001; Kearsley, 2000; Peters, 1998). Having knowledge of this component of remote learning does not help you determine the effectiveness of virtual learning implementation, how it influences the learner, or particular aspects that contribute to successful independent remote learning. The societal viewpoint of self-regulation offers an outline for virtual teaching and learning that can present understandings into the performance of self-sufficient students. Using this standpoint, Zimmerman (1989) characterized intellectual self-regulation as the degree to which pupils are meta-cognitively, motivationally, and psychologically committed to accomplishing their educational goals. Self-regulated students establish assignment-specific academic goals and utilize suitable approaches to achieve those objectives. They examine and assess their development and adapt their educational tactics when needed. They inspire themselves and continue to concentrate on attaining knowledge despite diversions. Students who have successfully been taught to self-regulate are able to request aid and make sure that their educational atmosphere is advantageous to their learning. In short, self-regulated learners are energetic and customizable architects of meaning, who take command of key facets of their intellect, actions, and atmosphere to help them attain their learning goals (Schunk, 2005). Zimmerman (1998, 1994) contends that a student's individual preference and ability to manage are distinguishing processes for self-regulation.

Lynch and Dembo (2004) identified five qualities of self-regulation which are essential for students to be successful during distance learning. The key qualities are pupil purpose, cyberspace self-assurance, the ability to command the clock, home learning atmosphere, and seeking online learning support. The characteristics of each key quality is discussed below:

Pupil Purpose

Pupil Purpose is the level of student motivation which includes the degree of self-reliance and the ability to set goals. When educators set the stage and provide an atmosphere which promotes a growth mindset, students begin to believe in their abilities, set goals, and persevere when confronted by obstacles. Students' ability to align their aspirations with their individual goals provide them with a sense of purpose and encourage them to succeed within the virtual learning environment. As educators, we must take time to discuss and model for students how we continue to persist when we are met with obstacles within the virtual learning environment.

Cyberspace Self-Assurance

The second quality that can be used to predict students' online success is based on each student's belief in their capability to perform the actions needed to generate specific outcomes within the virtual environment. This type of self-efficacy is contingent on a person's belief about their own actions, educational environmental atmosphere, and their level of motivation. According to Bandura (In Press), personal efficacy is the core belief and foundation of human motivation, well-being, and accomplishments. If a person does not believe they can deliver the preferred outcome through their actions, they will not be inspired to take action and endure when they are confronted with a barrier. If students do not believe in their ability to navigate through the online learning environment, they will have little hope or optimism to endure when they encounter obstacles.

Commanding the Clock

Palloff and Pratt (1999) noted that successfully navigating a Web-based learning program can take two to three times the amount of time that it would during a face-to-face environment (p. 73). With this in mind, both teachers and students may begin to feel overwhelmed. Teachers may be able to adjust to the longer periods of time needed to plan online learning experiences for their classes. Students, however, may find the amount of time very daunting and feel frustrated when they are not able to accomplish the tasks needed in an efficient manner. If their level of frustration is not addressed by the teacher, these students may stop attempting to complete their work entirely (Roblyer, 1999). Students' virtual learning tenacity is closely linked to both pupil purpose and cyber self-assurance. Students who believe in their ability to learn at a distance as well as setting and achieving goals will persist in working to manage their time efficiently (Gibson, 1998). Teachers should help students learn to assess the difference between easy and difficult academic tasks so they can prioritize them accordingly. Additionally, teachers should consider the amount of time a task takes within a face-to-face environment and multiply each task times two to determine the reasonable number of tasks students should be assigned to complete.

Home Learning Atmosphere

Students who have learned to manage their own time, goals, and learning will preemptively assess how their home learning environment should be set-up and adjust periodically when they find that it is hindering their ability to learn successfully online. When students are learning self-regulation, they are not yet equipped with this ability. It will be up to teachers to help students learn best practices and establish environmental protocols which best prepare them for class and learning each day. Whip and Chiarelli (2001) stated that students equipped with learning environment organizational approaches were more productive when learning virtually. To assist students in learning to self-direct themselves in this area, teachers should focus on helping students become mindful of where their learning space is located by questioning and helping them think about their home learning space. Possible questions include asking students things such as:

Is your space quiet?
Do you have books, workbooks, headphones, and supplies nearby?
Is there a place to charge your device if needed?

Questions like these model the internal questions students should ask themselves the next time they look for an optimal atmosphere to use for learning at home.

Seeking Online Learning Support

One aspect of virtual learning educators must remember is that learners often feel isolated from both the teacher and their peers. Just like in the face-to-face environment, students must be taught the procedure to follow when seeking help in the online classroom. This includes teaching students when, where, and how to seek assistance as well as deciding the appropriate resource to seek out. Self-efficacy includes knowing how other people can assist them with learning. One unique attribute of self-efficacy is a student's capability to obtain support to enhance their understanding of the technological system their school is utilizing. Educators should speak to students about the protocols to follow when seeking online assistance. We cannot assume that parents, relatives, or community stakeholders will be able to help students when their devices or online programs malfunction.

STOP & REFLECT

Let's consider the qualities of self-regulation and the impact they can have on student learning in the virtual environment. Take a look at the chart below. It illustrates the finding of Palloff and Pratt's research which notes that it takes a minimum of double the time allocated in a face-to-face environment to complete a task within the online environment. After reviewing the chart below, consider the last three tasks that you assigned students online. Then calculate the minimum amount of time it could have taken students to complete them during virtual learning. Add them to the chart below:

Task	Face-to-Face Environment (Time Allotment)	Virtual Learning Environment (Time Allotment)
Writing a summary of a text	20 minutes	40-60 minutes
Reading a chapter/ story in a textbook	Physical book- 14 pages 30 minutes	Electronically version-30-40 pages 60-90 minutes
Solving 12 Precalculus problems	36 minutes	72-108 minutes
1.		
2.		
3.		

After analyzing your calculations, what implications does this have for future planning and assigning of tasks virtually?

_____

_____

_____

_____

_____

_____

ADDITIONAL RESOURCES

Teaching Online -
A Six-Part Series:

Student Barriers to
Online Learning:

Barriers to E-Teaching
and E-Learning:

Teaching in the Online
Classroom by Doug Lemov:

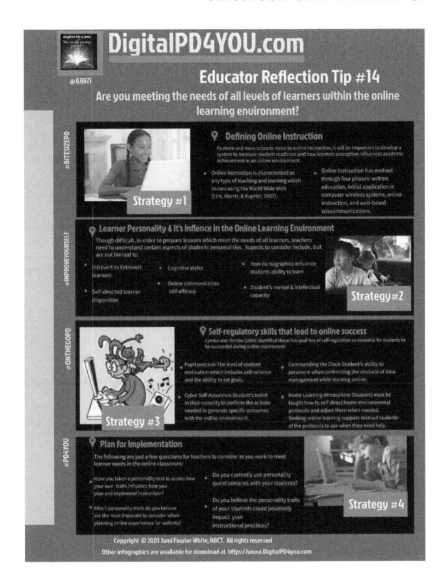

Infographics for each Reflection Tip are available for download at www. DigitalPD4You.com

Part II

Critical Literacies

"If we are not prepared to think for ourselves, and to make the effort to learn how to do this well, we will always be in danger of becoming slaves to the ideas and values of others due to our ignorance."

William Hughes

Reflection Tip #15: Are you teaching the "reader" or the "reading"?

When you read the title of this Reflection Tip, did you have to stop, think about it, and then go back and reread it? It is such a basic question, but critical to students learning to read. Over the past couple of decades, I have seen so many programs purchased, implemented, and showcased as the missing piece, the miracle fixer, or that last piece in the puzzle to help us produce proficient readers in our classrooms. Make no mistake. I believe that a core curriculum is absolutely necessary when teaching foundational reading skills

33

to children. I am not saying that teachers should not use these materials. I am asking that teachers think long and hard about whether so much time is spent making sure all of the components of the core curriculum are taught—- the content of a text, the central idea, the cause and effect relationship within the story, analyzing the character—- that we forget to focus on the *reader*. The intent of any reading curriculum is to educate students how to understand the text, not just grasp the content of the text, but to be able to utilize and apply the comprehension strategies that good readers instinctively use to facilitate constructing meaning from what they read (Boyles, 2004).

Most people don't remember learning to talk. It simply seemed to occur instinctively. On that same note, you likely don't recall much about how you were taught to read. Adults view reading as a seamless, uncomplicated, and automated process and may presume it should be a relatively simple skill for almost any child to develop. This, of course, is not the case. Learning to speak is an inherent capability supported by dedicated regions in the brain and is usually automated for children. Reading, for children, is a lengthy, complex task that entails years of deliberate purpose and practice. Teaching the brain to read necessitates a frequent and consistent routine of direct instruction. Children will not learn to read just by being in a room where reading is occurring. Direct reading instruction requires specific, intentional acts on the part of the instructor (Fisher & Frey, 2020).

Rosenshine's (2008) research on direct instruction yielded three major components to maintain a focus on students while teaching reading. The first is to reduce the complexity of the task when students initially begin to perform the skill by separating the lesson task into chunks. Secondly, teachers should model, and use think alouds to demonstrate specific strategies and thought processing when making choices and illustrating how to avoid common misconceptions. Afterwards, educators should use scaffolds and guidance to support pupils during their first attempts to practice the skill or concept being taught. Support can be as simple as listening to responses from all students to check levels of understanding and working through the task beforehand to help prepare and predict missteps that students may make. The last suggestion found within Rosenshine's research is to provide supportive feedback to students. The researcher describes feedback as including methodical corrections, rubrics or self-check lists, simulations of the finished task, and fix-up approaches (p. 2). If you truly want to focus on students during your feedback loop, consider reading about the E.M.P.O.W.E.R. Feedback Framework™ in Volume #1 of the *Educator Reflection Tips* series.

STOP & REFLECT

Answer the following questions:

Think: What processes are involved in the brain when we read?

Reflect. Why do you think reading is so difficult for some students?

Assess: How would you rate your content knowledge in regard to the ability to teach children to read?

Commit: Does your direct instructional framework for reading include all of the components suggested within Rosenshine's research? If not, which component will you begin to strengthen?

Reading & the Brain

> *The act of reading has existed for only 6,000 years or so---the blink of an eye when it comes to brain evolution. Human speech, on the other hand, has had 200,000 years to evolve.*
>
> ~Doug Fisher & Nancy Frey

When you open a book to read, the first thing that happens is that your eyes scan the wobbly lines and bends representing the letters of the alphabet and merge them into words as inscribed on the page. Next, specific areas of the brain work to correlate the written characters with the sounds of the language previously accumulated in your brain. Emergent reading ensues when segments of the left hemisphere of the brain which regulates working memory, verbal comprehension, and visual recognition are synchronized (Wolf, 2007). As these connections occur, other neural networks decipher the writing into a mental message that you comprehend. Amazingly, your brain can grasp and understand a complete sentence in a few seconds. It almost looks miraculous, but it is not miraculous at all. Reading is the outcome of an intricate procedure that includes decrypting nonrepresentational characters into sounds, then words that signify meaning. One of the remarkable aspects of the brain is its capacity to learn spoken language swiftly and precisely. We are born with the instinctive ability to discern specific sounds, known as phonemes, for all languages on the globe. Ultimately, we are capable of partnering sounds with capricious scripted symbols to convey our thinking and feelings to other people. Reutzel and Cooter (1996, 2000, & 2004) identified seven traits of effective reading instruction:

Language's Role in Reading

Being able to comprehend the role that language plays in the process of reading is an essential part of children's reading development. Reading is one of four basic language types: listening, speaking, reading, and writing. Highly effective reading instructors understand that the language arts are dependent on one another. Therefore, the ability to read is reliant on students having a strong listening and speaking vocabulary. Studies reveal that children who live in low socioeconomic environments begin school, on average, with only half the vocabulary of students who come from higher-income families (Healy, 1990). Hart and Risley (2003) further posited that "86 to 98 percent of the words recorded in each child's vocabulary consisted of words also recorded in their parents' vocabularies" (p. 6). The same research also implies closing the reading gap is assisted during schooling. The authors state that children can learn to read one million words per year in the school setting. The most effective teachers work to continuously find innovative and sustaining techniques to develop vocabulary and concept understanding in their classrooms.

Gauging Student Needs

The second characteristic of effective reading teachers is using reading assessments to inform instruction. Educators understand that in order to assist students they must figure out what skills students already possess and which skills they have not yet mastered, using these to plan appropriately-challenging instruction that meets the needs of the learners. Teachers perform a crucial role in assisting students with discovering their motivation to read and the delight of achieving (Duke et al, 2011). Great reading teachers also provide students with scaffolds needed to achieve success. This includes prioritizing both small group and individual assistance when applicable (Richardson & Lewis, 2018). Additionally, these teachers recognize that the best assessments are done across a period of time and evaluate prior and current capabilities. This results in the complete measurement of each student's progress.

Building Print-Rich Atmospheres

Well-organized learning spaces are arranged to stimulate the examination and contemplation of words and reading. Teachers fill the classroom with various types of print materials. They use "word walls, message centers, student work samples, lots of books from every genre, learning centers, and real world objects to inspire study and reflection" (Reutzel and Cooter, 2004, 2000, 1996, p. 7). Classroom structures should be thought through with an understanding that they are intended to convey learning as a strong component. The space design must invite conversation. Even in the absence of students, examining a teachers' classroom or virtual teaching space reveals qualities of each person's educational principles and standards. For instance, things such as the arrangement of the furniture and whether the word walls are visually engaging and academically appealing divulge whether the teacher believes in students learning through focused conversation and their beliefs about (Nichols, 2006). What does your teaching space convey to learners?

Instructional Toolbox

Teachers should have a wealth of instructional strategies to assist every student in reaching their maximum learning capability. Research-based strategies should be the pillar when planning for reading instruction. This pillar should include underlying components vital to teaching reading scaffolds. A few of the instructional elements for educators to include are listed in the graphic below.

Elements that lead to reading comprehension

Reading
Comprehension

Listening Comprehension
Decoding
Fluency
Strategies

Verbal Intelligence
Vocabulary
Preceding knowledge
Phonological awareness
Orthographic knowledge
Morphological awareness
Phonics knowledge
Cognitive Speed
Purpose

Source: J. Kelly (2007). Reading Comprehension:
Its Nature and Development. p. 4.

Explicit Modeling

Graves and Fitzgerald (2003) stipulate that effective teaching requires educators to increasingly perform a decreased amount of the work and for students to progressively assume increased responsibility for their own learning. It is during this practice of increasingly taking charge of their learning that students develop into competent self-directed learners. When introducing new knowledge, teacher modeling and additional support are essential. Modeling is defined as a teacher "demonstrating how a new skill looks when a competent reader uses that particular skill" (Reutzel & Cooter, 2004, 2000, 1996, p. 8). As students continue to develop the skill, they should take more ownership of their learning. Pearson and Gallagher (1983) coined this process as "gradual release" and it is especially vital when teaching and learning is taking place online. All students should be provided support at their instructional level at all stages of learning. It is imperative that we continue to do this regardless of the educational setting (Blackburn, 2020). As students begin to understand, efficient educators gradually release, allowing students to demonstrate the skill, while providing a great deal of support when needed. If you do not currently have a gradual release method to use when modeling instruction, I formed the **BRACE** method to help me remember the recommended features. It is illustrated in the figure below.

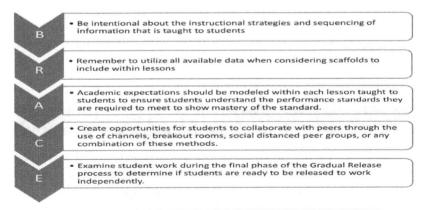

B
- Be intentional about the instructional strategies and sequencing of information that is taught to students

R
- Remember to utilize all available data when considering scaffolds to include within lessons

A
- Academic expectations should be modeled within each lesson taught to students to ensure students understand the performance standards they are required to meet to show mastery of the standard.

C
- Create opportunities for students to collaborate with peers through the use of channels, breakout rooms, social distanced peer groups, or any combination of these methods.

E
- Examine student work during the final phase of the Gradual Release process to determine if students are ready to be released to work independently.

- Educators should employ the "BRACE" method to help them remember to incorporate the Gradual Release process with students.

Family & Community Engagement

Parents and other family members have a profound influence on the development of a child's reading ability. Caviness (2020) asserts that "it's a common belief that parents are children's first teachers who play an essential role in a child's educational development" (p. 13 as cited in Fowler-White, 2020, p. 50). Efficient teachers encourage them to become active participants by encouraging parents to create home environments that stimulate the acquisition of vocabulary and a regular reading routine. These teachers also work to provide the families with strategies and resources that can be used at home to assist students in this area. Community stakeholders can be invited to assist the school by providing resources which can be used to increase student proficiency in reading or asked to volunteer to tutor pupils in this content area.

The Reading Reality

Currently, many students in the United States do not spend an abundance of time reading. In typical classrooms, pupils spend less than 20% of the Reading/Language Arts block reading (Brenner and Hiebert, 2010). Research indicates that a small amount of additional time makes a huge impact. Dedicating just seven more minutes each day to student reading has been shown to decrease the gap between those classrooms where students read well from those that students do not (Kuhn and Schwanenflugel, 2009 as cited in Hiebert, 2014).

STOP & REFLECT

Think about your current Reading/Language Arts block. What can you add/adjust/remove to ensure that students have an additional seven minutes to read during each class period? Reflect and write one commitment you will make to provide this time for your scholars.

Morning time, small activity, read. add in indep. Read Rotation.

Seven-minute Reading Commitment:

- Rotation time.
- Before school
- End of the day   last seven minutes
         ~~act~~ after Library
  outside reading

> *We need students who can do more than answer*
> *questions; today's complex world requires that our next*
> *generation of leaders be able to raise questions.*
> ~Kylene Beers & Robert E. Probst

Comprehending Complex Texts

Comprehension is essential in reading. Without deep comprehension, complex texts are lifeless objects. It is the reader's mind that gives a story life. It is astounding to observe the physical constraints of time and space fade away when a student participates in silent communing with an author through the act of engaged reading. As teachers of reading, we should work to routinely create experiences where students are able to engage in this type of silent communing with authors of all kinds.

In order for students to participate at this level, they must be provided with ways to access complex texts. Fisher and Frey (2013) note five access points for teachers to intentionally use to create linkage between the student and the text. These access points consist of:

1. Determining a purpose for reading a complex text and modeling how proficient readers construct meaning.

2. Supporting students with scaffolding and close reading instruction to steer students through complex texts.
3. Designing occasions for students to have collective conversations with their classmates to enhance their knowledge.
4. Pushing students further through individualized reading of progressively more complex texts.
5. Making use of formative assessment to help students see what they understand and are still working to understand. (p. xviii).

STOP & REFLECT

Within this Reflection Tip, various research-based strategies have been shared to encourage educators to focus on the reader instead of the reading. Use the tool in the Appendix C to help you examine your practice and pinpoint an area of need. Then create action steps to improve reading instruction inside your classroom

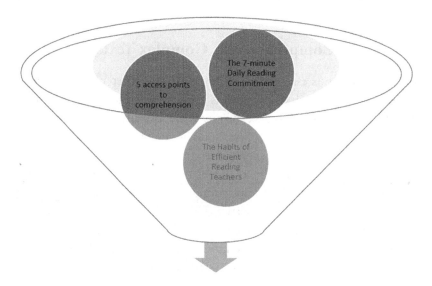

Reading Comprehension Experts

ADDITIONAL RESOURCES

The Reading Strategies Book by Jennifer Serravallo:

Rigorous Reading: 5 Access Points to Comprehending Complex Texts by Douglas Fisher and Nancy Frey:

How the Brain Learns to Read:

Structured Literacy - What You Need to Know:

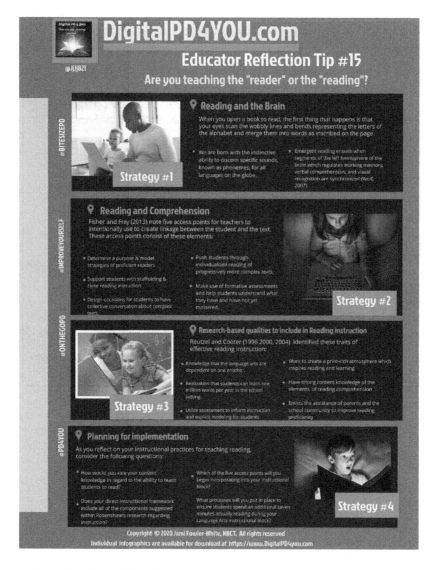

Infographics for each Reflection Tip are available for download at www.
DigitalPD4You.com

Reflection Tip #16: Is your classroom culturally competent?

> *"Culture, it turns out, is the way that every brain makes sense of the world. That is why everyone, regardless of race or ethnicity, has a culture. Think of culture as software for the brain's hardware. The brain uses cultural information to turn everyday happenings into meaningful events. If we want to help dependent learners do more high order thinking and problem solving, then we have to access their brain's cognitive structures to deliver culturally responsive instruction."*
>
> Zaretta Hammond (Culturally Responsive Teaching and the Brain, p. 22)

STOP & REFLECT

Before you begin this chapter, reflect on your personal expertise regarding culturally competent teaching strategies by answering the following questions:

1. What are your personal core values regarding equitable learning outcomes?
2. How do our personal beliefs about learning contribute to the barriers that exist within the learning process for students?
3. Define Culturally Responsive Teaching:

Educators have long contemplated strategies to aid in teaching students about diversity, specifically multicultural and racial topics, that would be beneficial in diminishing the impact of cultural divergence (Brown-Jeffy & Cooper, 2011). One topic of note that has formed in diverse teaching literature is culturally relevant pedagogy.

Ladson-Billings coined the term culturally relevant pedagogy in her book, *The Dreamkeepers,* in 1984. Her book discussed exemplary teachers of African American students. The pedagogy of opposition in the book examined the cultural disparity among pupils from culturally varied environments and their teachers, principally in circumstances of linguistic and verbal constructs. The view laid out within the book examined culturally based competence having its foundation in three postulations. First, learning should involve educational achievement. Second, teachers must refine and assist students in perpetuating discriminatory cultural competence. Lastly, scholars should be taught to sustain and embrace critical consciousness through which they question the status quo (Ladson-Billings, 1995; Johnson, 2007). Cooper (2003) amended the pedagogy and added that teachers should also hold high expectations for academic achievement and become the equivalent of secondary parents to students in their classroom. Additionally, Villegas and Lucas (2002) built upon the original premise and further suggested the following instructional practices be included within the framework:

1. Embrace social and political cognizance.
2. Uphold the viewpoint of pupils from varied backgrounds.
3. Hold themselves accountable for accomplishing change within the field of education.
4. Adopt a constructivist approach towards teaching and learning.
5. Use students prior intellectual competence and viewpoints as a basis for pushing their thinking towards the unfamiliar. (p. xiv).

Culturally responsive teaching (CRT), is a research-based approach which utilizes the ethnic qualities, encounters, and viewpoints of culturally varied pupils as instruments for educating them more proficiently. CRT is based on the beliefs that when educational knowledge and abilities are directly combined within the lived encounters and experiential facets of students, their influence is greater, learned with less effort, and understood more comprehensively (Gay, 2000). Our brains are wired to create links. It is easier for our brains to learn and store information when a connection is made. Traditionally, this is what pre-service programs have termed "background knowledge." Students come to our classrooms with everyday knowledge of their ethnicity, linguistics, and living experiences. By recognizing the gift that accessing background knowledge affords us, educators can tap into and create optimal learning environments for students of color and those from low socioeconomic populations. Generally, many approaches to culturally relevant or culturally responsive instruction designated in the multiethnic teaching literature endorse the application of students' culture as an agency for learning, while also cultivating an expansive social and political awareness which empowers them to evaluate the social norms, values, and organizations that generate and sustain social injustices (Ladson-Billings, 1995, p. 162).

Culturally responsive teaching strategies could be the key to scaffolding and supporting rigorous learning for diverse groups of students. (Breiseth, Garcia, & Butler, 2020). CRT could also serve as a mechanism for teaching students how to own their own learning and help to improve students' information-processing skills. The overall goal of culturally responsive teaching is to assist student development of cognitive processing skills and facilitate the growth mindset needed to leverage their neural pathways.

Perpetrating Cultural Expertise

Educators have always been told to use real-world examples and/or use students' background knowledge within instruction each day. Although this is the expectation, there is no uniform strategy or requirements for teachers to evaluate whether their current practices are effective. Below are ideas to help educators create culturally responsive environments:

- Shulman (1987) theorizes pedagogy as comprising subject matter knowledge, pedagogic knowledge, and educational content knowledge.
- Bartolome (1994) has criticized the search for the "right" teaching strategies and argued for an approach that includes civilizing

instructional practices which appreciates and utilizes the actuality, the past, and current viewpoints of students as an essential part of learning (p. 173)

- Wlodkowski and Ginsberg (1995) offer a four-part motivational context for culturally responsive teaching based on the theory of intrinsic motivation. This structure recommends that teachers and students repeatedly work to construct and refine four elements:

  1. An inclusionary atmosphere. Students and teachers should feel appreciated and connected while at school.

  2. Fostering a favorable outlook towards school. 3. Enrich the purpose of learning experiences by incorporating the ideals and viewpoints of students.

  3. Teachers must adopt the premise and recognize that student efficiency is increased when learning something they value (p. 19).

- Muhammad (2020) also proposes a four-layer equity framework: "identity development, skill development, intellectual development, and criticality" (p. 12). These elements are intended to signify the characteristics teachers should include in a culturally responsive classroom.

- Horsford, Grosland, & Morgan Gunn (2011) offer a structure for cultural relevance which begins with "political contexts, a pedagogical approach, a personal journey, and professional duty" (p. 594). This framework consists of examining the demographic divide, their own personal values, cultural competence, their approach to cultural relevancy and antiracism, along with their professional duty to lead with justice, commitment, and merit.

There are numerous vehicles educators can use to develop cultural responsiveness. I suggest beginning with the following four areas: cultural awareness, cultural elaboration, cultural expertise, and cultural divergence.

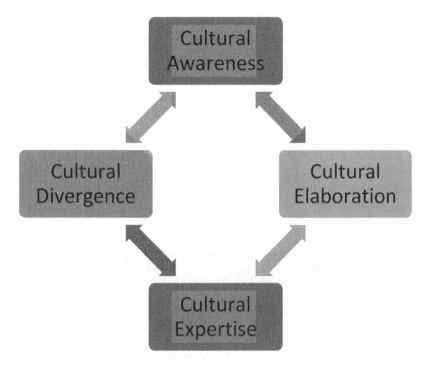

Adapted from Geneva Gray's 2002 article, Preparing for Culturally Responsive Teaching.

Cultural Awareness

Bias does not always have negative connotations. Simply put, it is an evaluation or belief that can be positive, neutral, or negative. Consider the following types of dessert:

Pumpkin Pie
Strawberry Pie
Blackberry Pie

Describe how you feel about them using the words positive, negative, or neutral.

If asked, I am positive about blackberry pie. When I was younger, each year my grandmother used to bake a blackberry cobbler for me on my birthday. Anytime I hear the word "blackberry," I automatically think of my grandmother and it brings a smile to my face. I find myself wanting to try any recipe or food that contains this type of berry. I have never eaten pumpkin pie, so I would say that I am neutral, due to having no context or background knowledge on this type of pie. In contrast, if offered a piece of apple pie, I would react negatively. I have never been a fan of the texture of cooked sliced apples, so these memories would not make me want to try a slice of this type of pie. Do you know what contributes to this negative reaction? This type of reaction is due to the mechanics of bias. Our brains are wired to categorize all aspects of our life.

STOP & REFLECT

Read the following quote:

> *For the most part, we do not first see, and then define, we define first and then see. In the great blooming, buzzing confusion of the outer world we pick out what our culture has already defined for us, and we tend to perceive that which we have picked out in the form stereotyped for us by our culture.*
>
> ~Walter Lippman

Do you agree or disagree with the quote? Explain your thinking:

Yes. I agree. I think we define first as a way of understanding or perhaps as a way to control the our understanding.

Eberhardt (2019) uses apples to explain the mechanics of bias. In Chapter 2 of her book, *Biased*, Dr. Eberhardt asks readers to think about apples. Close your eyes for thirty seconds and think about apples before continuing to read.

This category contains all the beliefs you have about how apples grow, where they grow, what variations exist, the colors that they come in, how large they are, what they feel like, what they taste like, when we should eat them, whether you will choose to cook them, cut them before you eat them, or eat them raw and whole. Along with this, it also influences whether you will eat an apple when someone offers it to you, buy one at a store, or pick one at an orchard. Think about the pictures or preconceived thoughts, images, and feelings that popped into your head when you were asked to think about the apples category. The stronger the feelings and thoughts that you have associated with this category; the faster the thoughts come to mind. Just like in the example with apples, implicit biases creep into our everyday actions and influence our behaviors, both inside and outside the classroom. Implicit bias can affect our decisions, behavior, and perceptions. The term implicit bias was first created in 1995 by psychologists Mahzarin Banaji and Anthony Greenwald. They contended that social behavior is predominantly influenced by unconscious bias, negative associations that people unknowingly hold. They are expressed automatically, without conscious awareness.

Cultural Elaboration

Cognitive research reveals that the brain ignores information until it is made relevant. Teachers should work to contextualize content and assist students with activating schema. One way this can be accomplished is through the use of various common cultural learning tools. The most common cultural learning tools for processing information utilize the brain's memory systems, that assimilates songs, echoing, metaphor, chants, tangible maneuvering of subject matter, and routines. Using these strategies shows students that teachers are responsive and accepting of the cultural capital and tools they bring to the classroom (Hammond, 2015; Aguilar, 2015). Learning tools that cross cultural barriers and have the highest effect sizes are included below. As you examine them, take note of one of these areas that you would like to begin integrating into your next unit of study.

Perspectives .85 effect size	Talk & Word Play .82 effect size	Puzzles & Patterns .67 effect size	Memory .67 effect size

Cultural Expertise

Culture consists of numerous factors. Educators should be aware of those that have direct connotations for instruction. Connotations that could impact instruction are ethnic groups' cultural principles, rituals, modes of communication, learning styles, influences, and social patterns. Specifically, teachers may need to consider whether an ethnic group gives importance to shared living and collaborative problem solving and how these penchants affect students' motivation to learn. Students' ambitions, potential academic performance, and how diverse ethnic group etiquettes affect how children intermingle with adults and gender socialization unveils itself in classroom settings in terms of things such as equity initiatives. This constitutes the first essential component of culturally responsive teaching (Gay, 2002). After considering student cultural tendencies and traditions, educators will need to begin to systematically introduce these cultural scaffolds progressively to aid in skill acquisition.

Cultural Divergence

The culture and ethnological identities of pupils and their teachers continues to signify a demographic divide (Milner, 2007), while also expanding the stages of cultural divergence, which arise when scholars experience incongruity between the culture built at home and school (Delpit, 1995; Gay, 2000; Hale-Benson, 1986; Ladson-Billings, 1994). In certain circumstances, this divergence culminates in cultural struggles (Delpit, 1995), cultural conflicts (Beachum & McCray, 2004; 2008), and, in more worrying situations, the practice of cultural complicity, where teachers indirectly exclude students from a culture that is not outwardly acknowledged and appreciated in the school (Beachum & McCray, 2004). Even though this may be inadvertently exhibited by teachers, it can manifest itself in several ways within schools, especially when educating students of color.

Native American educator Cornel Pwewardy (1993) asserts that one of the reasons Native American children struggle in schools is that educators customarily have endeavored to inject culture into instruction, as a replacement for implanting education into the culture. Culturally relevant teaching necessitates students retaining some cultural honorableness in addition to educational superiority. Fordham and Ogbu (1986) noted the phenomenon called "acting White," where African American students worry about being shunned by peers for exhibiting inquisitiveness in and prospering in academic aspects within schools. Other researchers have offered differing explanations of this behavior. They denote that for many African American pupils, school continues to be a foreign and antagonistic locale. This antagonism is discernible in the tailoring and stance that the school snubs (King, 1994). As a result, an African American student wearing a hoodie in class or baggy pants may be punished or ridiculed for their clothing choices instead of explicitly exhibited behaviors. This has caused students of color, especially African American students, to perceive school as a place where they are required to conform and not truly be themselves (Majors & Billson, 1992).

STOP & REFLECT

Do your students feel comfortable being themselves within your classroom? What measures do you use to ensure that you do not possess any implicit biases which may result in students feeling uncomfortable being themselves? Before continuing this chapter, consider taking the self-assessment linked here to assess and address any implicit biases you may unknowingly possess: https://implicit.harvard.edu/implicit/takeatest.html

ProdigyGame.com offers a list of culturally relevant teaching strategies to help educators begin to build their expertise in this area. The list below comprises strategies from this website as well as my own insights. As you read through the list and the examples, begin thinking about your students' cultural and ethnic backgrounds and whether these strategies parallel students' lives outside of school:

1. **Know Your Students**: Being accessible and communicating frequently with students can help you discover students' preferred learning styles.
   Suggested classroom practices: Collaborative discussions, providing surveys, questionnaires, and team building activities.

2. **Individual Consultations with Pupils**: Talk to students during non-instructional time. Question them about their interests, hobbies, get feedback about prior lessons, and their favorite classroom activities.
   Suggested classroom practices: Choose students to talk to when the class is at the restroom, greet students at the door with a question of the day, visit students during lunch, talk to students during recess.

3. **Context Matters**: Find innovative ways to integrate students' culture as a frame of reference for students during instruction.
   Suggested classroom practices: Revise word problems, case studies, use real-word phenomena that have cultural context for students, and allow time for students to discuss or talk to you about the connections they made to the content of the lesson.

4. **Use Student Vernacular/Home Language**: Explaining terms using vocabulary or the home language of students activates their schema, captures their attention, and immediately helps their brains begin working to connect the new information and prepare to store it in their long-term memory.
   Suggested classroom practices: Use lyrics from familiar songs, create multilingual vocabulary walls, and provide examples using familiar places in the school community.

5. **Make a Real-World Connection**: Invite community stakeholders to speak to the students to demonstrate the real world application of the skills/concepts students are learning.
   Suggested classroom practices: Scientists, Engineers, Architects, Computer Technology Specialists, Farmers, Accountants, and so many more people can be invited to speak to students. Virtual speakers should also be considered. This offers limitless possibilities for creating opportunities for students to connect with the content.

6. **Capitalize using Gamification**: Think about the properties of gamification and how they appeal to students. Students work harder to level up, attain badges, and earn points in the gaming world. How could you use these attributes within lessons?
   Suggested classroom practices: Propose projects where students create games for their peers, write instruction manuals, have students collaborate in teams or work individually to move through different levels. Reward students with points, certificates, or badges as they progress through each level.

7. **Peer Instruction/Collaboration**: Many cultures support the common practice of generations teaching one another. Consider assigning projects which require students to discuss, teach, and learn from each other.
   Suggested classroom practices: Use the Jigsaw method, classroom presentations, collaborative group work where students are assigned questions and allow time for the students to ask and answer questions with peers.

8. **Enlist Parents:** Provide parents with newsletters or some form of communication that provide them with information about an upcoming unit. *Suggested classroom practices*: Ask parents to assist, supply real world examples, pictures, or record short videos explaining cultural items to provide context to be used during instruction.

STOP & REFLECT

Think about your classroom. Then complete the following steps:

A. List culturally responsive practices that you are currently using.
B. After creating your list, categorize your practices under each of the four elements provided in Appendix I.
C. Analyze the final categories to determine an element that you will work to strengthen.
D. Use a different color pen to add 2-3 strategies you will commit to integrating under the category you will work to strengthen.

ADDITIONAL RESOURCES

Culturally Responsive Teaching (Understood.org):

Culturally Responsive Teaching (ASCD):

Culturally Responsive Teaching and the Brain by Zaretta Hammond:

Biased by Jennifer Eberhardt:

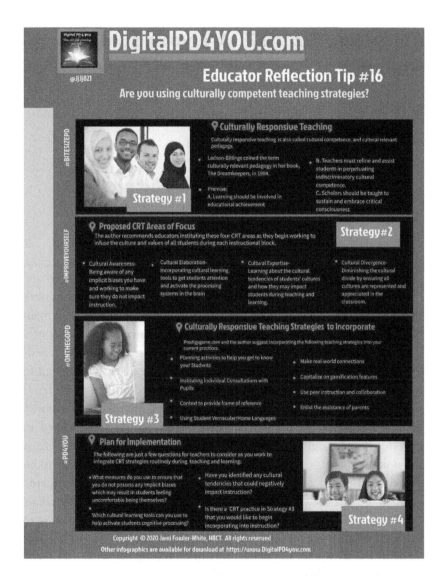

Infographics for each Reflection Tip are available for download at www.
DigitalPD4You.com

Reflective Tip #17: Are your students practicing "good" digital citizenship?

"Our kids are exploring a new frontier. Largely, they're playing on digital playgrounds and no one is on recess duty. That has to be us."

Kevin Honeycutt (Staff, 2016)

Digital communication has transformed the methods that we use to communicate in the world. In their book, *Teachers Deserve It*, authors Hughart & Welcome emphasize that in 1800 a mailman used to deliver a large bag of letters to businesses once a month. Although the information was obsolete by the time it was received, people were grateful to receive it because it was the only way they had to communicate. In today's fast-paced system, we need only to pick up our smartphone and we can instantly connect with people all over the world. Due to these advancements and many others, we no longer need to operate solely within the community in which we reside. Everyone fears the unknown, but as educators it is our duty to teach our students to effectively use the latest technological advances so that they are prepared to operate with the ever-growing digital world (Hughart & Welcome, 2020). In 2017, Bill Gates reported that the average age for students to receive their first smartphone was ten and that fifty percent of these students would have a Social Media account by the age of twelve (Curtain, 2017). It is incumbent upon us to add discussions to our instructional practice which help students become digitally literate and increase their ability to use digital technologies while simultaneously understanding the implications of those actions.

STOP & REFLECT

Have you considered the type of content or resources you will use to teach your students the non-negotiables of good digital citizenship and safety when learning online within your instructional lessons? List the top three digital literacy topics that you think children need to know about:

1. _____
2. _____
3. _____

What exactly is digital literacy?

If you examine the history of the term, you find that it continues to evolve as new technological tools are introduced. Let's take a look at the history of this term:

- Walter Isaacson posits that because technology allows students to solve problems across disciplines, educators should rethink not only *what* we teach our students, but *how* we are teaching them (Isaacson, 2014).
- Ribble (2015) defines digital citizenship as an idea for helping students learn to link respect, education, and online safety by encompassing nine norms. These norms include: digital etiquette, digital law, digital access, digital rights and responsibilities, digital literacy, digital commerce, digital rights and responsibility, digital safety, and digital health and welfare.
- The International Society for Technology in Education, (ISTE), defines digital citizens as pupils who use technological tools responsibly with compassion to help make the planet safer. They divide digital citizenship into five domains: inclusive, informed, engaged, balanced, and alert. The *inclusive* domain involves students exhibiting respectful behavior in online communities and practicing empathy. *Informed* digital citizens examine the accuracy of content to check precision, viewpoint, and authenticity.

While *engaging* online, digital citizens should be committed to community engagement and use good judgment. Digital citizens should also be taught about balancing their time. Students will need to learn how to make decision-making, be responsible, and prioritize their time online. Essentially this means teaching students about working to find a *balance* between their online and offline activities. Lastly, ISTE (2018) suggests that students should practice *alertness* in the online world. This incorporates staying safe and creating harmless places for others.

- Common Sense Education states that the purpose of digital citizenship curriculum should be "to equip young people with the knowledge and skills they need to navigate the digital world as well as the disposition and agency to ensure they put those skills to use" (Weinstein & Mendoza, 2019. p. 9). The authors go on to divide digital citizenship into six topics which include: media balance and well-being; privacy and security; digital footprint and identity; relationships and communication; cyberbullying, digital drama, and hate speech; and news and media literacy.

As you consider each definition, remember that digital citizenship is more than just making sure students know how to use the latest technological tools; it must include equipping students with problem solving skills and the ability to choose the proper tool to use to help extend their knowledge (Becker et al, 2017). Regardless of which definition you believe fits what you would expect a digital citizen to exhibit, it is important that students understand how to navigate the digital world, be given the opportunity to practice using technological platforms, be expected to understand and abide by online etiquette, taught that things occurring virtually are not imaginary, and that a person's digital profile and social media biography are often the first place people examine when they want to learn more about other people. The 2017 NMC Horizon Report offers these strategies for promoting Digital Citizenship:

- **Fostering Authentic Learning Experiences**: Digital Citizenship promotes integration of technology into instructional experiences, instead of teaching students how to use digital resources in isolation. Teachers should immerse students in experiences that will help them become digital Interactors by incorporating digital news and media literacy, digital laws, digital commerce, and digital rights and responsibilities.

- **Provoking innovation and collaboration**: Educators should encourage students to work collaboratively both in person and during remote learning experiences. This will require teachers and school leaders to create unique experiences that may not have been previously used. By combining technology and innovation, students will be better prepared to seek and find solutions when they encounter unforeseen obstacles in the future. When we teach students the proper way to collaborate online, it will help them to learn about digital etiquette, cyberbullying, and digital health and wellness.

- **Use Storytelling and Situational Exercises**: As you work to help students understand all the digital citizenship characteristics, consider using storytelling and situational exercises to help improve students' critical thinking skills and digital knowledge. Stories and experiences can help to foster ingenuity as students realize they need not be experts when they begin using technology. When coupled with situational exercises, students will be able to put into practice things such as determining the reliability of online sources, using age-appropriate websites, and the importance of privacy settings.

- **Increasing Access**: Students should be able to learn wherever they are. Therefore, teachers can help to promote digital citizenship by advocating to school administrators and district leaders for the purchase of digital media which can be used to enhance the learning process for students. Along with this, educators should also be open to allowing students to use these media as much as possible.

In his book, *Innovators*, Isaacson (2014) notes that advances in technology have revolutionized the way we live, but for our students technology is the norm and has and will remain a constant part of the way they learn, communicate, and work. As educators it is crucial that we not only teach our students how to use technology, but make sure they understand how to use it safely. One strategy that can be used to groom students for a future that is ever changing is to pose digital scenarios and have an open discussion about the pros and cons of each possible response. An example of a Grade 5-12 scenario follows: *Ethan has stopped hanging out and talking to the other students at school. Instead, he spends 6-8 hours on his online gaming system on school nights and sometimes up to 14 hours during the weekend. You have tried reaching out to him through text or phone calls, only to be told that he is in the middle of a game and will call you later, but he never does. Since you and Ethan have been friends since Kindergarten, his mother reached out to you because she is concerned about him withdrawing from social settings. During her phone call, she stated that he refuses to pause the game to come down and eat dinner with the family or talk to relatives when they visit their house. His mother was wondering if Ethan was still communicating regularly with you or if he has also isolated himself from his friends as well.* After reading the scenario the teacher can pose questions to provoke student reflection and discussion. Within the discussion, students should be required to use evidence from the scenario to support their choice. Using such scenarios can help students internalize the characteristics of digital citizenship and help them to develop real world problem-solving skills.

STOP & REFLECT

Before you determine which characteristics of Digital Literacy you would like to adopt for your classroom, be sure to review your district's policies related to online media usage to help you prioritize which aspects of Digital Citizenship to focus on. Afterwards, use the graphic organizer in Appendix E to begin to craft the Digital Citizenship components that you will work to integrate into your classroom culture.

ADDITIONAL RESOURCES

What Students Need to Know about Digital Citizenship:

Nine Resources for Teaching Digital Citizenship (ISTE):

5 Creative Ways to Teach Digital Citizenship:

Digital Citizenship (Age-Appropriate Strategies):

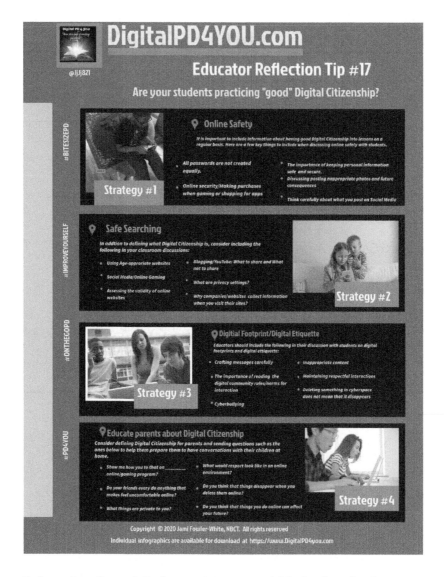

Infographics for each Reflection Tip are available for download at www.
DigitalPD4You.com

Part III

Cyber Connection

Reflection Tip #18: Technology: Friend or Foe?

"Our generation, and that of our children, will face its share of crisis just like every generation in the past. When those calls come, will you be ready? The answer depends on how we educate the next generation."

Oliver DeMille

Teachers as Technological Immigrants

Year 3 of my teaching career was full of surprises. One day my principal, Mr. Jordan, rolled a large cart that had a television and a desktop computer attached to it into my class and said to me, "I don't know how you are going to do it, but I want you to begin using this to teach." As a teacher, I was always overjoyed when I received any new tools, but this one came with no training manual and I was expected to begin using it immediately. Reflecting back to that time in my career, it parallels what many educators went through during the sudden school closures in March 2020. As technological immigrants, our mindset about integrating digital tools into classrooms may be quite different from students who have been immersed in technology since birth. In his book, *Empowering Students with Technology*, author Alan November depicts an image of a student reaching high to get a book off of a bookshelf while standing on a desktop computer. This depiction was intended to shine a light on the nearsighted view that educators had towards technology. It was being used as more of a step stool for teachers to keep teaching just as they had always done. Instead, the authors were suggesting that educators should adopt a type of long-term vision, enabling them to see new technology as a means of enriching instructional practices (November, 2001, p. iii). As we continue to reimagine teaching and learning, educators must work to adopt a growth mindset and begin to recraft a vision which includes how technology can be used to inspire our students to strive for excellence.

Prensky (2001) identified the subsequent attributes of both digital immigrants and digital natives. The variances are exemplified by inconsistencies in the way they converse and the way they use digital technologies and language.

Digital Immigrants	Digital Natives
Adopters of web technology	Born during or after the influx of technology
Rational learners	Spontaneous learners
Concentrate on one assignment at a time	Quickly switch between tasks and/or multitask
Prefer to talk to one person at a time	Very social; Revel in being around a lot of people.
Get information from traditional news sites	Continuously on their phone or another technological device.
Prefer communicating in-person	Prefer using social media or other apps to communicate

(Unicheck, 2015, Riegel & Mete, 2018)

STOP & REFLECT

How do you measure up? Do you have more characteristics in common with Digital Immigrants or Digital Natives? Consider the following questions:

1. Were you born after 1997?
2. Are you an intuitive learner?
3. Do you favor multitasking when completing assignments?
4. Are you a person who likes to communicate with an audience or multiple individuals?
5. Do you prefer retrieving news from a digital device?
6. Is it your preference to use technology and apps to communicate?

If you have answered "Yes" to most of the questions, then you are on the road to the "Digital Native" way of learning.

If you answered "No" to most of the questions, you are more likely a "Digital Immigrant" as a learner. Regardless of your answers, reflect on the question below:

Which area do you need to strengthen in order to complete your assimilation into the digital native way of thinking and learning?

_____

_____

_____

_____

Contemplating the Needs of Digital Natives

More often than not, initial studies advise that digital natives who do not have formal instruction in regard to computer literacy skills are inadequately inept when compared with peers who have been taught computer literacy skills in a course at school (Brock, Thomsen, & Kohl,

1992; Karsten & Roth, 1998; Gho et al, 2008). The job market is drastically changing at such a precipitous pace that it is vital for schools to undergo transformation in spite of the challenges. After all, we are setting the foundation for the next generation of lawyers, doctors, scientists, and political leaders (Sheninger, 2014). Students crave personalized technology-infused learning experiences. Instead of thinking about the barriers, opposing views, or potential obstacles, educators should embrace a take-no-prisoners approach and impose technology-infused strategies to help students grow and excel. For the purposes of this chapter, personalized learning is defined as "teaching techniques that integrate technology with one-to-one tools in order to assist all students with achieving at high levels of learning" (Grant & Basye, 2014). Engaging in personalized instructional practices enables students to use technological skills that they likely already possess while catering to their individual gifts, academic needs, and interests. It also allows students to take ownership of their learning paths. Moving to personalized learning practices will require a major shift in school structures to help set students on a path towards demonstrated proficiency in 21st century-skills such as communication skills, working in partnership with others, the ability to solve complex problems, use self-corrective thinking, and ingenuity through the formation, ingesting, operation, and distribution of digital content for the purposes of being able to think and work to solve their own problems (Grant et al., 2014; Beers, 2011). When educators begin to move towards a sort of equilibrium between face-to-face and digital schoolwork, they are creating an opening for personalized learning and increasing the probability of success for every learner, irrespective of background and academic differences.

Teach Me How to Validate and Socialize Academically Online

In the age of the internet, everyone is free to publish their own versions of practically anything. Digital natives need to know how to sift through the information they find and determine if it is authentic. It is our job to make sure that students are prepared for the world. Being digitally literate includes being able to not only navigate through the massive amount of information that is available, but also learning to use digital tools to communicate as well. Without knowledge of these two key skills, students will be left behind and forced to depend on other people to interpret for them. Have you been teaching your students to be communication and information literate?

In addition to communication and information literacy, students will also need to master the art of communicating digitally. This includes being able to send and receive emails, navigate video conferencing tools, and successfully use social media tools common within the business world. Along with learning to use these tools, students will also need to be taught how to work collaboratively to solve real world problems using technology. In recent months, businesses have moved towards a virtual work environment. Are your students prepared to thrive socially and work in teams in this type of digital environment?

Consider Integrating Gamification Benefits

Stephen Johnson's (2006) research has shown that when students participate in student-directed learning, as they do when working to master video games, they are able to build cerebral aptitudes and increase their overall IQ in ways that books are not able to cultivate (Johnson, 2006). To progress through the levels requires balancing complex patterns, hand-eye coordination, and a multitude of things such as shifting landscapes, visual cues, internalized maps, and memorizing numerous button combinations to control character movements. You don't often hear about the benefits of gaming. Most times, we only hear how addictive games are. Did you know that online games are addictive due to them connecting with the reward circuits of our brains? (Johnson, 2005).

Though we will discuss this topic more in-depth in Volume #3, let's take a closer look at two more cognitive benefits of gamification. One benefit is that students engage in experimentation while engaged in gaming. To effectively complete a task in a game, students use the inquiry method to chart a path of success. This teaches students about the benefit of learning from their mistakes and helps them to develop a growth mindset. The second advantage of gamification is tiering. Gaming also teaches students to focus on a series of hierarchical missions as they work to achieve an objective. This demonstrates to children the benefit of aiming for short and long-term goals concurrently. These two practices require a series of decision-making processes which incorporate evaluating data, scrutinizing circumstances, and refer to their overall goals.

Lastly, students gain processing skills through gamification. In education, we talk about having students adopt a growth mindset. Gamification is the growth mindset in action. My son, DeVon, and I recently discussed the benefits of gamification. Within our discussion, he stated that he loves that online gaming promotes risk taking and learning from mistakes. In contrast, he argues "that the educational system does not promote this type of thinking. It instead punishes students when they fail which encourages them to believe that mistakes are horrible." The mistakes students make should be used as an opportunity to decipher students' thinking. Students should be taught to learn from their mistakes. As I observe teachers, I am always looking for an opportunity to help them learn and grow. Sometimes this involves reflecting when goals are not achieved. My son went on to explain that in his experience, students are taught to believe that schooling is all about making A's and passing tests instead of truly focusing on learning. Finally, our discussion concluded by DeVon praising his AP Physics and Geometry teachers for their use of the process of self-correction. After completing an assessment, his teachers have him self-correct his work which he says bridges the gap between his mistakes and mastering the standards.

Find a Balance Between Analog and Digital Experiences

Today's youth are passionately embracing digital tools, while some from older generations are not as attuned to their use for learning. As a result, a divide is created between students who are enthused about using these digital tools and applications and educators who are having difficulty integrating these types of technology and grappling with the necessity to continue using these types of technology throughout instruction (Lui, 2010). College 2.0 defines Web 2.0 tools as free digital tools that can be used to create and share student-generated projects, products, and content. These tools are interactive, have multiple purposes, encourage collaboration, and are easy to use (Gulley & Thomas, n.d.). These tools allow students to move beyond static web content and engage with other people around the world. Some of the more popular educational Web 2.0 tools are YouTube, Flipgrid, Google Docs, Blogging platforms, See-Saw, GoAmimate, and WeVideo. (Liu, 2010). McCoog (2008) stated that twenty-first century instruction requires teachers to create a sense of equilibrium between the lesson objectives and the academic needs and feedback of students. Additionally, the author suggests that we rethink the "three R's" that were popular when most of us were in elementary schools. People used to emphasize Reading, wRiting and aRithmetic. There has been a move in the 21st century towards the three R's which focuses on "Rigor, Relevance, and Real-world skills" (McCoog, 2008, p. 3). Schools must be equipped with essential Information and Communication Technology (ICT), including curriculum and resources designed to promote collaboration and student-centered settings (Boholano, 2017). This type of curriculum and digital resources will foster environments students can relate to, encourage their participation, and will help them develop the skills they need to be productive citizens in the world. Although the goal is for Digital Immigrants to assimilate into the world of Digital Natives, Riegel and Mete (2018) suggest that Digital Immigrants help their students learn the following:

- How to continue learning when technology fails.
- Understand the importance of personal interaction.
- How to recognize nonverbal cues.
- Assess the shortcomings of specific types of technology and how to use traditional research methods such as books, journals, and newspapers.
- How to work on tasks to completion instead of beginning multiple tasks all at once. Be sure to stress that sometimes working on multiple tasks simultaneously might cause them to get distracted.

STOP & REFLECT

How does your digital literacy toolbox measure up?

Explore the Web 2.0 tools in Appendix G. Which three tools do you think will be the most beneficial to your practice? List them here.

1.
2.

ADDITIONAL RESOURCES

Bridging the Digital Divide in
the COVID-19 ERA:

Gamification: A Teen's
Perspective:

College Star: Web 2.0
Engagement Tools:

*50 Powerful Web 2.0
Tools for the Classroom:*

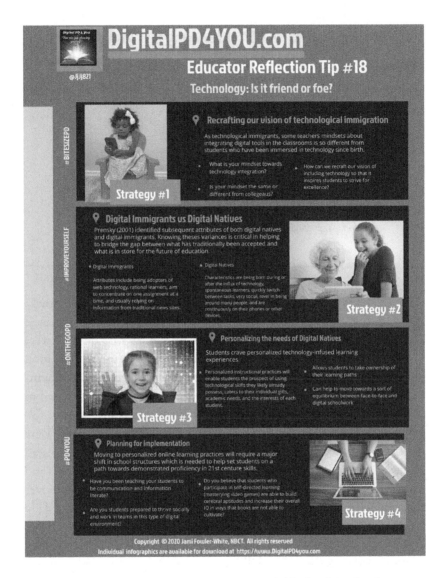

Infographics for each Reflection Tip are available for download at www.
DigitalPD4You.com

Reflection Tip #19: Have you adopted the principles of learning theory in your virtual classroom?

"Technology is just a tool. In terms of getting the kids working together and motivating them, the teacher is most important."

Bill Gates

Historically, technology in some form has been a part of teaching for nearly a century. Overhead projectors, initially used for military training purposes in the 1930's, quickly were integrated into schools. As new technologies were created, education integrated them into classrooms—film projectors, calculators, typewriters, and televisions were some of the early technology resources used in schools. Then in 1984, the first Apple computer was introduced, followed by SMART Boards in 1991. Twenty-first Century Grants were bestowed on schools for teachers to use for instruction--which consisted of a large cart with a television, computer, and VCR. Today, teachers and students use laptop computers, iPads, and tablets in classrooms all over the nation. Technology is a valuable resource and can be effective in daily instruction. Many researchers have focused primarily on the technical aspects of using these new technologies within the educational environment instead of pedagogical skills necessary for using the technologies.

The COVID-19 pandemic has placed a spotlight on virtual instruction, commonly called online learning, as many of the nation's schools have been forced to close in an effort to keep students and educators healthy. When tackling the topic of online learning, research focuses mainly on blended learning, which is a combination of face-to-face and online instruction. This seems to imply that online learning is a subset of the traditional environment instead of focusing on virtual learning as its own construct of learning. Therefore, the information gathered, while necessary and valuable, generally lacks a pedagogically relevant theoretical underpinning and has not generated advances in teaching/learning theory that have served to benefit both virtual teachers and learners (Phipps & Merisotis, 1999). This chapter will attempt to connect the research on virtual learning with pedagogical strategies which will help educators capitalize and become more adept at creating an effective virtual learning environment for all students. Let's explore variables and learning theories that may contribute to teacher and student success within the online environment.

Stop & Reflect

As you read about each learning theory, take note of the principles that you most identify with or are considering incorporating into your current practice. Appendix H can be used to keep track of the ideas for each of the learning theories discussed in this chapter.

Learner Variables & Theories

The research on learning theory is intended to enlighten us about the way people learn. These theories depend on several disciplines including sociology, neuroscience, psychology, and education. Theory is described as declarations, values, or concepts associated with a specific subject matter. In the field of education, various theories are embedded in teacher preparation courses to ensure pre-service and in-service teachers have a foundation to differentiate instruction in the classroom. The knowledge gained from these theories arm educators with techniques, strategies, and best practices to provide instruction for all students. In a typical classroom, a variety of learning styles are common, as no two students will learn or think alike. This doesn't change when instructing virtually. It is still incumbent upon the teacher to assess their classroom and construct effective lessons for the learning styles of the students in order for them to achieve academic success. When reflecting on the myriad of learning theories, there are several that continue to impact instruction today:

Learning Theory #1: Behaviorism

Behaviorism concentrates on how individuals act. Specifically, how performance generates responses. Within the field of education, behaviorism assesses how pupils conduct themselves while being taught. This includes observing how students react to specific provocations that when duplicated can be calculated, measured, and ultimately regulated for each person. The primary focus centers on the visual instead of mental processes. This theory of behavior is often associated with Ivan Pavlov's famous dog and food experiment.

John B. Watson is credited with coining the term behaviorism. Watson contended that the brain and awareness is inconsequential in the educational process. He states that what most influences behavior is the overall effect of past experiences, specifically whether they were positive or negative (Catania & Laties, 1999). Behaviorism also stresses the usage of both positive and negative reinforcement to facilitate people learning new behaviors, establishing habits, and—with the introduction of computer assisted instructional model—replication to boost optimistic learning pursuits. Behaviorism became the primary basis for the taxonomy created by Benjamin Bloom (1956), commonly referred to as Bloom's Taxonomy. Bloom's Taxonomy became the basis for other widely used frameworks such as Webb's Depth of Knowledge and Costa's Levels of Questioning.

Garrison, Archer, and Anderson (2000) created a model of online communities inquiry. This model asserts that two forms of presence are required in the online community. The first is teacher presence. It is discussed in Reflection Tip # 20. The second is cognitive presence. Cognitive presence is described as "the extent to which participants in any particular configuration of a community of inquiry are able to construct meaning through sustained communication...{it} is a vital element in critical thinking" (p. 4). When we look at Bloom's Taxonomy, Webb's Depth of Knowledge, and Costa's Levels of Questioning, each can be used to help educators create this sense of intellectual presence due to each outlining qualities needed to increase the intellectual rigor of academic tasks.

Learning Theory 2: Cognitivism

Bloom's Taxonomy laid the groundwork for cognition to become the focus of learning theory. Cognitive psychology originated from the Latin word "cognoscere" which refers to finding out or ascertaining (Katsev, 2013). This theoretical context of understanding the mind emerged in response to behaviorism's exclusion of cognition in its theory. Cognitivism supports the idea that the brain has a vital part in learning and concentrates simultaneously on a learners' reaction to an environmental stimulus. Cognitivist theorists view the mental operations of the mind, such as inspiration and creativity, as essential aspects of learning which link environmental stimuli and learner responses.

This theory has two main mechanisms, one mechanical and the other theoretical. Operationally, cognitivism embraces a positive methodology and the idea that psychology can be, in theory, entirely expounded upon through conducting experiments and the scientific process. The operational component hinges on the belief that the intellectual structural design can be pinpointed and subsequently comprehended. The second is the belief that cognition involves distinct inner intellectual conditions, interpretations, or emblems whose influence can be explained as algorithmic rules or formulas. This learning theory became a dominant force of psychology in the 1950s as an extension of Behaviorism, which acknowledges that mental states exist (Fernando & Marikar, 2017).

Two decades after the introduction of Bloom's Taxonomy, Robert Gagne, developed another taxonomy which became the basis of cognitivist instructional design:

Gagne's Nine Events of Instruction are illustrated in the table below.

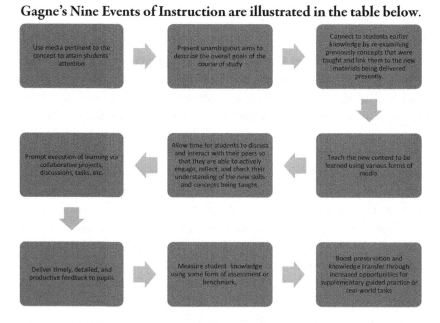

Adapted from (Ngussa, 2014)

Each of the events within Gagne's model identifies mental conditions for learning. There are specific mental stimuli which each event aims to evoke in the learner. Educators should work to include each of these aspects within their virtual classrooms. The first event is intended to evoke or stimulate receptions in the brain to get students ready to learn. While talking to students about the objective, the intent is to set an expectation for students to learn within the lesson. What processes are you currently using to get students' attention at the beginning of each lesson that is presented online? Activating prior knowledge is encompassed for the purpose of arousing and retrieval of short-term memory processing within the brain for students. As the teacher begins to deliver content to students, teachers aim to provide students with a careful preview of the skills and concepts to be learned. Guided practice is a critical aspect of the online learning process. This aspect sets the stage for long-term memory to be activated and learning to become permanent. As students are released to work independently within the synchronous environment, students are able to translate and authenticate their understanding of the content. It is important for teachers to provide timely feedback as a way to support learners and to help evaluate correct execution of the concepts and skills being completed by students. What does your online feedback loop look like? After students practice, teachers should assess students to conduct one final check for understanding, and lastly, when possible, assign students a real-world task to solidify retention and ensure students will be able to transfer and apply the new learning to other circumstances. Are you using a coordinated system of exit tickets to check for understanding? Online programs such as NearPod afford teachers the opportunity to actively engage students, assess their knowledge, and provide real-time feedback (van Glaserfeld, 1995).

Learning Theory #3: Constructivism

There is no single constructivist theory. The Constructivist methodology is predicated on multiple research principles (Paris & Byrnes, 1989). Even though knowledge in one sense is intimate and individualistic, students build understanding by interacting with the natural world, collectively working within community settings, and in a social and academic atmosphere. Within constructivism, learning is a process of using personal experiences to build understanding (Sjøberg, 2010). In a constructivist classroom, the teacher's central responsibility is to solicit and generate dialogue. Steering students through the process is intended to serve as a catalyst for students producing their own questions and conclusions about a given topic (Sjøberg, 2010).

There are several derivatives of this learning theory. Social Constructivism articulates the depiction and rationalization of teaching and learning as an intricate, interactive social phenomena between teachers and students. Four of the most popular social constructivism theories were created by Lev Vygotsky, John Dewey, Jean Piaget, and Howard Gardner. Vygotsky theorized that learning is analytical and the social construction of explanations to problems Vygotsky explained the learning process establishing a "zone of proximal development" in which the teacher, the student, and a problem to be deciphered exist. Essentially, Vygotsky defined the Zone of Proximal Development as the distance between what students can do individually on their own and what students will be able to do in the near future with the help of a teacher or in partnership with more competent peers (Picciano, 2017, p.170). Social constructivism also stresses that teachers furnish a social environment for students to collaboratively manufacture the knowledge needed to resolve problems.

Similarly, John Dewey thought of learning as a sequence of useful social experiences in which students learn by being actively involved, working in partnerships, and surmising with others. Although his theory was developed in the 1900s, Dewey's work and practices are evident within today's social constructivist instructional design. The use of reflective practice by both student and teacher is a pedagogical basis for collaborative conversations, regardless of whether learning takes place in a face-to-face or online environment.

Jean Piaget centered his learning theory on four phases of cerebral development which begins at birth and lasts through a child's teenage years and beyond. Piaget emphasized creating social, interactive communities for students, with the teacher serving as facilitator. Within these interactive communities, students should be expected to work through complex challenges while investigating social problems, mathematical and science expressions, or case studies.

STOP & REFLECT

Describe how you are using or will use collaboration and reflective thinking with your students:

Promoting Collaboration & Reflective Thinking:

Learning Theory #4: Connectivism

Thus far, the learning theories shared have centered on the learner; technology is never mentioned. In Connectivism, learning is a process of connecting points or information sources. This learning theory is dependent upon technology and understands the role the Internet and technology play in helping people expand their knowledge. This model of learning recognizes key shifts in the pathways from which knowledge and information arise, expand, and vary. Internet technology has pushed learning from inner, individualist actions to collaborative clusters which work to link specialized interrelated activities. Within Connectivism, students are required to comprehend and participate in experiences related to circumnavigating and realizing the continuously shifting and advancing informational systems (Picciano, 2017). In 2004, George Siemens (2015) recommended eight principles of connectivism to guide educators in creating these types of experiences for students:

1. Learning and understanding lies in a variety of views.
2. Learning is a means of uniting specific points or information suppliers.
3. Learning might be located within non-human applications.
4. Learning involves the capability to understand beyond what is presently known.
5. Cultivating and sustaining relationships is necessary to enable constant learning.
6. Capacity to realize relations among disciplines, concepts, and philosophies is a fundamental competence.
7. Precise and up-to-date understanding is the aim of Connectivism learning.
8. The ability to make decisions is a knowledge-seeking method. Selecting what to learn and the connotation of inbound data is glimpsed through the view of an ever-changing existence. The readily available right answer now, may be incorrect tomorrow when new information which may influence the decision is collected.
   (Adapted from Figure 5. Siemens' Eight Principles of Connectivism by Picciano, 2017, p. 185)

STOP & REFLECT

Siemens asserts that learning involves diverse opinions, adopting the premise that students can learn from various types of technology, connecting ideas, and using the most current information possible within lessons. Are you currently using these or any of the other principles of Connectivism? Match one of your classroom practices with each principle described above. If you are unable to think of an example, use a different color pen to create a strategy that you will pledge to embrace:

Principle	Classroom Practice which illustrates this principle of Connectivism
#1	
#2	
#3	
#4	
#5	
#6	
#7	
#8	

As technology continues to transform the way educators look at teaching and learning, another learning theory has emerged within the last decade. The Online Collaborative Learning (OCL), was created by Linda Harasim and touches on the capabilities of the Internet to support learning conditions which nurture partnership and the construction of knowledge. Harasim (2012) defines OCL as "a modern theory of learning that redesigns conventional and non-conventional education for the Information Age using the Internet" (p. 81). The OCL theory contains three phases of knowledge construction through collaborative partnerships where learners create ideas, shape ideas, or unite knowledge. This theory is derived from social constructivism which encourages educators to take the role of facilitator and allow students to solve complex problems by interacting with peers. When implementing this level of collaborative learning, the teacher facilitates the process of constructing understanding. This theory is most successful in classrooms that have a low student-teacher ratio.

Within the virtual environment, depending on the age and readiness level of your students, connectivism theory practices may be the most difficult to implement. All educators know that students need to collaborate with each other. True collaboration requires teachers to wholeheartedly adopt the role of facilitating learning. In this role as facilitator, educators will need to emphasize helping students learn to navigate through the online platforms which often proves to be much harder than within an in-person setting. Some teachers will also need to tackle the more complex undertaking of executing hybrid models which couple both in-person and online pupils who need to collaborate with each other. Even when students are ready for this type of collaboration and begin to circumnavigate it, teachers are encouraged to set up systems to manage student accountability and monitor learning within collaborative settings online.

Crafting an Effective Virtual Learning Environment

A virtual learning environment is thought of as either a subset of learning or a subset of distance learning. To date, the most well-respected theory describing effective virtual learning environments speculates four intersecting points of view. Bransford, Brown, and Cocking (1999) surmise that educators include these four aspects within virtual learning experiences with students. These aspects are civic consolidation, centralized learning, targeting students, and using focalized assessments.

- **Civic Consolidation**- This aspect consists of norms that encourage collaboration and learning. This facet is based on the premise of teachers not only creating a community within their classrooms, but a level of understanding which includes knowledge of the influence outside factors can have on student achievement. Along with using this knowledge to engage and improve experiences for students, teachers should also invite the community in (both in-person and virtually) to assist with the improvement of student achievement and infuse the use of technology to help them build relationships with parents and solidify the home-school connection.
- **Centralized Learning** -This area is tied closely to teacher knowledge. When teachers learn to use new technology, they model the learning process for students and begin to attain new intuitions

by observing students learning. Many students are also intrigued by the new tech and will, in turn, spend hours working to learn to use these tools on their own and will attempt to become more proficient than both their peers and teachers. Since both teachers and students are novices, the creation of knowledge is a truly collaborative venture (Bransford, Brown, and Cocking, 1999, p. 226-27).

- **Targeting Students**- Children have innate biological capabilities for learning. Learning is supported and controlled by the child's ecology and atmosphere. The brain of a growing infant is impacted both by biological and ecological influences. Development in these terms is crucial to understanding the changes in children's intellectual evolution. Intellectual variations are not the end result of ordinary accumulation of knowledge but are due to procedures entangled in abstract restructuring. Research from many fields has presented important conclusions about how initial cognitive capacities correlate to learning. With this in mind, consider the impact the classroom community, students' background, life outside of school, and the overall school environment has on students' ability to learn. Are you promoting student centeredness within your classroom? Is it promoted school-wide? If not, what processes need to be put in place to create this type of atmosphere? (Bransford, Brown, and Cocking, 1999).

- **Focalized Assessments**- Assessment and feedback are critical elements of learning. In a focalized assessment environment, tests should mirror instruction, happen continuously, and provide information to students, teachers, and parents. Additionally, assessments should reflect the quality of students' thinking and the specific content they have learned. Factors such as the purpose, nature, content, task demands, and cognitive level are among the criteria which teachers should use to examine the level of focalization in the area of benchmarking and assessments (Bransford, Brown, and Cocking, 1999, p. 245).

As you plan to implement these practices consider the following questions:

1. What methods are you currently using to build community within your classroom?
2. Do you offer opportunities for students to share their knowledge of technology with you and their peers?
3. Are you promoting student centeredness in your classroom?
4. What criteria are you using to ensure assessments measure students' quality of thinking?

STOP & REFLECT

Based on what you just read regarding the four intersecting points of view for virtual learning experiences, how would you rate your implementation in these four areas? Give yourself a rating of Advanced, Proficient, or Novice for each area below. Then write a commitment statement describing the actions you will take to strengthen the area with the weakest rating:

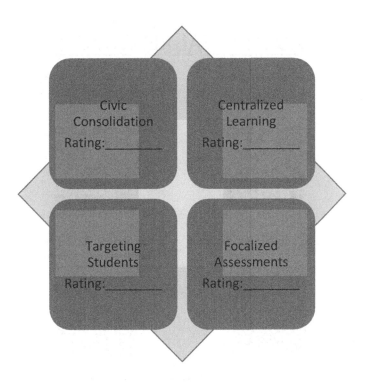

Civic Consolidation
Rating:_____

Centralized Learning
Rating:_____

Targeting Students
Rating:_____

Focalized Assessments
Rating:_____

Commitment:

_____
_____
_____
_____

ADDITIONAL RESOURCES

Learning Theories: Four Major Ones for the Classroom:

Learning Theory and Instructional Design/ Technology:

Learning Theory: Instructional Resources:

Overview of Learning Theories (Berkeley.edu):

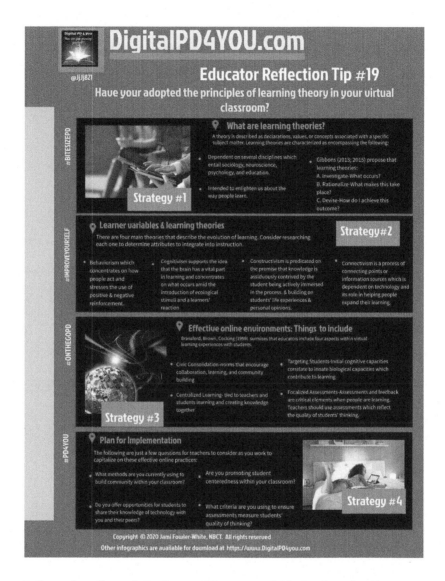

Infographics for each Reflection Tip are available for download at www.
DigitalPD4You.com

Part IV

Classroom Culture

"Student engagement is the product of motivation and active learning. It is a product rather than a sum because it will not occur if either element is missing."

Elizabeth F. Barkley
(Student Engagement Techniques: A Handbook for College Faculty)

Reflection Tip #20: Are you using positive engagement strategies with students in remote or hybrid learning?

Each year, educators spend time trying to figure out how to increase student engagement efficiently and consistently. As we continue to examine customary methods used to engage students in the traditional school setting and attempt to revise or revamp them for hybrid and remote learning, it is imperative we begin to develop a common language around what exactly constitutes student engagement. Traditionally, engagement is defined as time-on-task, but this is just one of the essential aspects involved in student engagement (Brophy & Good, 1986). There is an abundance of literature listing examples of activities and strategies to increase student engagement. However, the Center for Comprehensive School Reform and Improvement points out that although positive student engagement is a crucial factor to consider when working to increase student achievement, it is not as widely discussed in research as other factors such as data-driven instruction, leadership at the school level, or teacher qualifications. Additional definitions of student engagement include the following:

involvement in academically efficient methods, within and beyond the school room, resulting in a variety of quantifiable learner outcomes (Kuh et al., 2007).

- the degree to which students are participating in actions that research has shown relate to effective educational results (Krause and Coates, 2008, p. 493).
- the value of effort students themselves devote to instructionally focused tasks that assist precisely in the achievement of anticipated results (Hu and Kuh, 2001, p. 3).
- establishing for pupils a feeling of fitting in through participation, commitment, and kinship (Kift and Nelson, 2005).

Engagement and Active Learning

There is no doubt that educators spend an inordinate amount of time mapping out engagement strategies which will be used throughout lessons each day. Before teachers can focus on student engagement, however, they must determine which type of engagement they are focusing on. Engagement is more than commitment or input. It entails emotions and understanding as well as actively learning (Harper & Quaye, 2009, p. 5). Working without emotionally engaging is simply conformity; emotional connection without performing is disconnection. Fredricks, Blumenfeld & Paris (2004) pinpoint three elements of student engagement:

Emotional Engagement

Students who connect emotionally feel sentimental responses such as interest, enjoyment, or a sense of belonging. Essentially, emotional engagement can be defined as the amount of care students feel when they are taking part in the classroom learning community. This can be measured by asking students if they feel valued, observing how students intermingle with their teacher and peers, assessing whether students are pleased with their teacher, measuring the level of family engagement, and monitoring how students respond emotionally.

Behavioral Engagement

Students who are socially engaged characteristically obey societal norms, such as attendance and participation, and refrain from disruptive or undesirable behavior.

To determine if students are behaviorally engaged, teachers should assess how long students are actively engrossed with the lesson materials. Teachers can examine this by looking at how long students spend on modules/assignments virtually, using the number of times they log into the online learning platforms, completion of tasks, and their level of participation in class discussions.

Cognitive Engagement

Cognitively engaged students are devoted to learning, pursue activities that are above the expected requirements, and enjoy intellectually demanding tasks and assignments.

Educators should pay close attention to how students connect to what they are learning. This type of engagement can be measured through student execution of classwork and assessments, as they interact and discuss with peers, and through written tasks in online platforms such as NowComment within virtual settings (Fredricks, Blumenfeld & Paris, 2004, p. 62-3, as cited in Trowler, 2010). NowComment.com is an online platform which allows teachers and students to upload texts, images, or statements. The texts, images, and statements can be annotated and used to springboard one or several discussion threads simultaneously. Simulated activities such as these help to promote connection, community, and engagement within an online environment.

STOP & REFLECT

Now that you have learned about the three domains of engagement. Let's reflect on the six key criteria from the definitions of engagement that have been used to describe what it should look like in the classroom.

Part #1: Decide which type of engagement (Emotional, Behavioral, or Cognitive) is represented by each of the descriptions below:

A. _____

B. _____

C. _____

D. _____

E. _____

Part #2: How are you cultivating and measuring student engagement in your classroom?

1. Valuing Effort

Strategy for cultivation	Criteria to measure this type of engagement

2. The Degree of Student Participation

Strategy for cultivation	Criteria to measure this type of engagement

3. Time-on-task

Strategy for cultivation	Criteria to measure this type of engagement

4. Involvement in academic tasks

Strategy for cultivation	Criteria to measure this type of engagement

5. Establishing a feeling of fitting in through participation, commitment, and kinship

Strategy for cultivation	Criteria to measure this type of engagement

Motivation as a vehicle for engagement

If we think back to the quote that began this chapter, we are reminded that student engagement is two-fold. We have discussed the components of active learning; let's take a deep dive into the connection between motivation and engagement. According to Pink (2009), genuine motivation is a by-product of three distinguishable intrinsic components. These three key components are Autonomy, Mastery, and Purpose. In his book, *Drive*, the author defines each of these internal incentives as follows:

Autonomy is the aspiration to oversee one's own life and direction. Pink indicates that people need to feel liberty in one or more of these four aspects of life which I have dubbed the 4 C's. They are chronology, classwork, course of action, and connections.

- *Chronology* equates to a person having the choice to decide at what time they work, the extent of time they spend on a project, or the regularity at which they take on new assignments. When a limit is placed on the amount of time that students can spend on tasks, projects, or to achieve an objective is set by others, it diminishes their enthusiasm regarding the work.
- The second C is *classwork*. People would rather have the option of deciding on activities and assignments rather than having them assigned. Whenever possible, teachers should allow children this level of liberty.
- The third is *course of action*. For course of action, people can select *how* they accomplish a goal. In this level of liberty, people likewise desire choice regarding the measures, approaches, and strategies used to complete a task.
- *Connections* implies that people feel liberty when they can choose with whom they collaborate. Partnerships awaken people's natural ability to be self-motivated.

Mastery is the push to accomplish a mission and continue to work to get better. People work hard when they believe they are working on something important that has meaning. In this type of liberty, people are often so engaged in working towards the goal that they move about in a sort of rhythm and glide through the duties instinctively and before you know it have achieved a goal. Pink (2009) outlines three tenets to achieve this type of liberty in the school environment. The first tenet is to focus on children's mindset. Mindset is a person's mental attitude. Steve Maraboli says, "Once your mindset changes, everything on the outside will change along with it (Hall, 2017). Refer to Reflection Tip #13 to learn more about helping students learn to have a growth mindset. As educators, it is imperative you survey students to determine their beliefs regarding ability, effort, and goal-setting. The way a person answers each of these and many other questions can determine a person's mindset and beliefs about their own ability, and how they feel about effort.

The second tenet is pain endurance. Let's face it, if any of this were easy, everyone would achieve their goals. The truth is that there will be countless obstacles along the way on most learning endeavors. It will take an intense amount of effort, and an abundance of time to accomplish many of the goals that we aspire to achieve. Teachers will need to help children learn about sociologist Daniel Chambliss's "mundanity of excellence" (Chambliss, 1989). Chambliss argues that success does not take a tremendous amount of talent. Instead, he maintains that excellence is humdrum. One can achieve excellence through the accomplishment of many minor, mundane, everyday tasks that we perform with automaticity. When fused together, these minor tasks create a whole. These automatic tasks help us reach the level of mental stasis needed to be innovative and accomplish the goal, find the solution, or achieve the result we are seeking.

The last tenet of self-sufficiency is reaching for infinity. In mathematics, an *asymptote* is defined as "a curved line that comes haphazardly close to infinity but never reaches it." (Pink, 2009, p. 41). When the goal is to always get better while accomplishing an objective, you will never stop working to attain this level of self-sufficiency.

Purpose is the last of the three intrinsic components of true motivation. It is classified as the longing to do service in hopes of achieving something larger than ourselves. When people have mastered the first two intrinsic motivators and combine them with a feeling of support for a big idea, there are no limits to what can be achieved (Pink, 2009).

To create positive student engagement in your classroom, consider merging these strategies:

A. **Attainment Mindset**: Student mindset should be an emphasis for all educators. When students are not taught to use growth mindset strategies, they will be incapable of attaining high levels of academic engagement after encountering small obstacles. Therefore, teachers should educate students about metacognitive strategies, talk to them about identifying their "fixed mindset triggers", and celebrate effort and learning from mistakes/failures. These things will encourage students to continue to work towards goals.

B. **Unwavering Support**: In times of change, students may be reluctant to ask for assistance when they don't understand something or when they make mistakes. The mistakes are often compounded when they are unsure how to navigate new technology, are learning a new strategy, or getting to know a new teacher. Teachers will need to work to reduce this awkward anxiety and intimidation by providing unwavering support and positive reinforcement. This can take on many forms. For example, students can be given oral acclaim and special acts of esteem when goals or milestones are met (Coomey & Stephenson, 2001).

C. **Purposeful Objectives**: Children need to be provided with clear, consistent, and focused goals. Lesson objectives should be defined to help students understand what they are working to achieve. Objectives and goals help students feel connected and engaged with the content being taught. When connecting to a big idea, an overall goal can be recognized. After this happens, children can begin to feel that their work is valued. This recognition inspires dedication and hard work (Coomey & Stephenson, 2001).

D. **E.M.P.O.W.E.R. Feedback:** This element of student engagement is two-fold. First, it is important for students to know that their teacher welcomes and appreciates the effort that they put forth to complete an activity, task, or project. This can be demonstrated to students through a strong feedback loop. The E.M.P.O.W.E.R. FeedbackTM framework which was first introduced in Volume #1 has seven characteristics:

A. **E.M.P.O.W.E.R. Feedback™:** This element of student engagement is two-fold. First, it is important for students to know that their teacher welcomes and appreciates the effort that they put forth to complete an activity, task, or project. This can be demonstrated to students through a strong feedback loop. The E.M.P.O.W.E.R. Feedback™ framework which was first introduced in Volume #1 has seven key characteristics:

E - Empower students with feedback on their progress towards meeting the expectations of an academic standard

M - Merge the idea of constructing feedback with the student and standard in mind

P - Provide personalized next steps to students

O - Orient toward a goal collaboratively set by both the teacher and student

W - Work to help students take ownership for their learning

E - Employ every opportunity to give personalized feedback framed to improve academic progress

R - Routinely used by the teacher to shape teaching and learning in the classroom

(Fowler-White, 2020, p. 76-77)

Implementing the E.M.P.O.W.E.R. Feedback ™ Framework will help students stay focused and guide them towards mastery of standards and learning goals. In addition to teachers valuing students' effort, students should also be taught to value their own effort. Brain research teaches us that when we learn to appreciate our own progress towards a goal, it generates changes in our brain which make us feel happier.

E. **Collaborative Community:** Students need to feel like they are part of a collaborative community. This entails a feeling of fitting in. Teachers can help to achieve this type of classroom culture by committing to the academic development of all students, ensuring that all students are able to participate, and planning learning experiences which help students to build authentic kinship with their peers.

Societal Atmosphere

Since most of the world is teaching at least in part online at the time I write these words, the last section of the chapter will focus on actions teachers can take to generate positive and engaging connections between students in a virtual environment. Researchers have written about the necessity to establish a societal atmosphere of teachers and pupils throughout virtual instruction. A societal atmosphere is "the phenomenon that helps translate virtual activities into impressions of real people" (Dixon, 2010. p. 2). It can be created through observable acts, such as group tasks, when students send and respond to messages from their peers, offering choices within lessons, and other classroom protocols intended to remind everyone that other people are occupying the space with them (Kehrwald, 2008, pp. 94-95). Teachers must create this type of atmosphere in the virtual space. According to Paris (2008), a societal atmosphere can be accomplished by combining three elements. These elements are *capability, prospect*, and *impetus*. The first is the *capability* of participants to send and read societal atmospheric cues. *Prospect* refers to creating opportunities for students to intermingle with each other. People crave personal associations. Personal collaborations should be organized and devised to foster beneficial connections, avert students from being overpowered by the strains of networking within the whole group setting, and create a sense of harmony between the need for malleability and the required lesson framework (Coomy & Stephenson, 2001). *Impetus* is the desire to interact with other students. This does not happen by chance. Students need to understand why participating in these interactions are advantageous for them (Kehrwald, 2008).

Questions to consider when planning engagement interactions for lessons:

What criteria will you use to measure the cognitive, behavioral, and emotional engagement of students?

How will the engagement strategy support student mastery of the skill/concept within the lesson?

Have I surveyed students to determine their interests, attitude about effort, and academic goals for the year?

Which aspects of societal atmosphere are you currently using with students?

STOP & REFLECT

Use the tool in Appendix I to help you craft a plan to solidify student engagement by reflecting on the characteristic of societal atmosphere you would like to strengthen and constructing classroom protocols that will increase or help students positively engage during remote or hybrid learning settings.

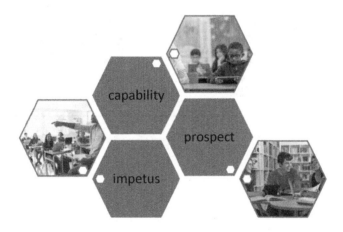

ADDITIONAL RESOURCES

131 Tools for Distance Learning and Student Engagement:

Using Positive Student Engagement to Increase Student Achievement:

How Intrinsic Motivation Helps Students Manage Digital Distractions:

Teach Like a Pirate by Dave Burgess:

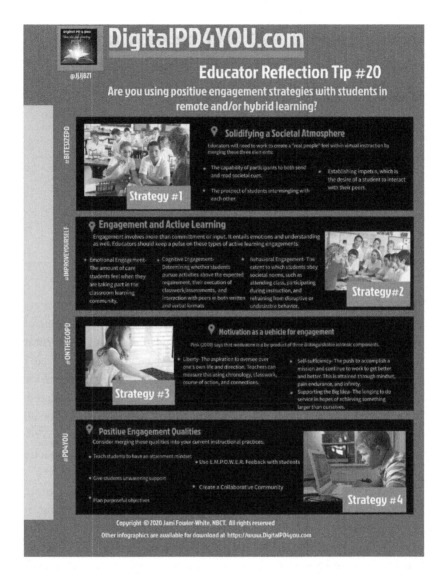

Infographics for each Reflection Tip are available for download at www. DigitalPD4U.com

Reflection Tip #21: When navigating change, do you believe that peace is a choice?

"The oldest and strongest emotion of mankind is fear, and the oldest and strongest kind of fear is fear of the unknown."

H. P. Lovecraft

No one likes the feelings that come when we think that we are not in control. In this particular time in society, it often seems as if we are NOT in control. With this in mind, it is important to reflect on our current practices in regard to navigating change. I can't imagine how our students are feeling, but I know that as educators, we will not be able to help students if our own emotions are not regulated. In the early 1900s, psychologists began to define intelligence based on an intelligence quotient (IQ), which measures a person's cognitive capability and performance. Performance largely focuses on someone's capacity to understand, remember, use, think, justify, and explain the abstract.

Mayer, Salovey, & Caruso (2004) classify emotional intelligence (EQ) as the ability to make sense about feelings to enrich thinking. It incorporates the capacity to correctly understand emotions in an effort to retrieve and produce reactions that will support thinking, to comprehend feelings and emotional expertise, and to thoughtfully control feelings to foster emotions as academic development (p. 197). Emotional intelligence is a core component of the overall intelligence of humans. In essence, emotional intelligence focuses on the sensitive, intimate, social, and survival scopes of intellect. These aspects are in many cases more vital for everyday operations than the "conventional" aspects of intelligence. This is partly due to the fact that emotional intelligence is tactile and correlated to current operations while cognitive intelligence is calculated and associated to long-term capacity. A person's EQ helps to predict success because it reflects how a person applies knowledge to an immediate situation. In a way, emotional intelligence can be thought of as assessing a person's common sense and capacity to get by in the world (Grayson, n.d.).

Why is emotional intelligence important?

Life doesn't come with a built-in GPS system. Our emotions, which range from uncontrollable anger to passionate feelings of love, are what our bodies use to send instantaneous alerts and signal changes within our world. These responses keep our internal and external worlds synchronized, which allows us to remain safe and continue to thrive. Giving in to our natural guidance system will be useful to us if we give in to it, but sometimes our emotions are not as dependable as we would like for them to be. Sometime when we work through similar situations, our emotional responses include visual memories which influence our perception. The outcome can be beneficial or detrimental, depending on our emotions. Feelings such as rage, embarrassment, and nervousness can suppress growth. Over time a person's emotional reactions in certain situations can begin to run on automatic pilot. When we lose sight of these signals, the result might be a lack of reaching our full potential in life (David, 2015).

Imagine going swimming in a lake. As you are wading through the water, you may be hesitant to just close your eyes and start to swim since you are not sure how deep the water is or whether the current is fast or slow. Due to this, you continue to push your way through the water very deliberately and move only a few feet away from the bank. Similarly, when people are not sure of the outcome, they tend to do what is most familiar to them, routinely going through their day and refusing to venture out past a certain point. This fear of the unknown causes us to set limits and prevents progress.

Psychologist and author Daniel Goleman outlines five essential elements for attaining emotional intelligence (2015):

- **Recognizing Self**: According to Goleman's research, recognizing self is the ability to identify your emotions and in what manner your responses, tone, and behaviors affect others. Being aware of yourself also includes understanding the connections among the things you are feeling and how they perform. In this element, you are cognizant of your area of strength and those you need to improve. You are receptive to innovative ideas and events and use collaborative experiences with others to learn and grow (Cherry, 2020). In order to know yourself, you must first examine how you react in situations and understand what you believe in. For example, if you tend to lash out at others when you are stressed, then you may need to find a method to help lessen or adjust your emotions during stressful periods.

- **Self-Management**: This facet incorporates the ability to evaluate one's feelings and actions. It includes the ability to use verbal and non-verbal forms of communication precisely and regulating thoughts while pursuing long term goals. Managing emotions does not mean taking a stance where you don't show your emotions. It just means that you take a moment to stop and think about the impact your emotions will have on situations and choose the appropriate environment and time to articulate them. When a person masters self-management, they are able adjust and accommodate when change occurs. Self-management is deeply rooted in a person's principles and social integrity. A person's values can help to dictate their actions, where they spend time, how they react in situations, and how they respond to others. As you continue to self-reflect, determine whether you struggle in this competency. If so, consider sitting down and creating a list of what you value. This is a good place to begin working to self-manage emotions. Traits of self-management include: persevering when confronted with barriers, remaining adaptable, learning to calm yourself down when you get upset, and having focused goals (Gore, 2002).

- **Social Intellect**: Being able to connect and interact socially with other people is essential. This involves more than just regulating your emotions and understanding their impact. For educators, social intellect also encompasses forming relationships and getting along with colleagues, parents, school leaders, students, parents, and community partners. Characteristics of a person who has social intellect include: possessing efficient listening and conversational competences, being able to balance who they are and how they are perceived by others, and resisting the urge to start a dispute when someone contradicts your point of view (Morin, 2020).

- **Compassion for Others:** The ability to empathize about how other people are feeling is vital to obtaining social intelligence. Assessing a situation and responding with compassion can positively impact social interactions in all settings. Correctly being able to construe the emotional tendencies and responses of those we come in contact with on a regular basis helps us develop and sustain relationships.

- **Plotting Your Purpose:** External motivators like fame, money, and acclaim tend to become barriers to success when they are not attained. When plotting your purpose, it is important to prioritize internal motivation over external incentives. By working to gain internal rewards, people have a larger sense of goals and greater opportunity to seek social intelligence. Being competent in this area requires attributes such as being task-oriented, setting goals, being driven and determined to succeed, looking at mistakes as opportunities to improve, and a high level of devotion to work towards what they aspire (Cherry, 2020.)

Changing your emotional trajectory

Change can be difficult because it can challenge how we think, how we work, the quality of our relationships, our physical security, and our sense of identity. If you examine the research regarding change, you will find that there are two ends of the change spectrum. One end contains avoidance or attempting to escape the process of coping. The opposite end involves controlling and accepting change. In order to figure out where you are on the continuum, let's look at the stages of change.

The *Prochaska and Diclemente's Principles of the Change* process consists of the following six stages:

1. **Baffled Disbelief:** The first stage of change is characterized by disbelief, denial, and a feeling of bafflement. Within this stage, people often question why things are changing, work to preserve what they thought of as normal, and build a wall of resistance to avoid the change. This lack of awareness stems from a belief that their life cannot be improved by changing.

2. **Deliberation:** This stage involves acknowledgment of the dilemma, preliminary reflection on a performance or life adjustment, and collecting data about potential resolutions and next steps.

3. **Meditation:** Within this stage, people are expected to reflect on the decision to change, including the necessity to modify performance or alter life experiences, and take a definitive look at proposed action steps to change.

4. **Execution:** In Stage 4, people should work to implement the actions that were reflected on within the meditation stage of this process.

5. **Upkeep:** During stage five of change, people must commit to the behaviors introduced during the meditation stage.

6. **Closure:** The last stage brings closure and realizing that the former problem behaviors or past experiences are no longer desirable.

When you begin to examine where you are within this continuum, it is important to understand the benefits of working through the process as quickly as you can. These benefits include the fact that you will feel healthier. Even a minimal amount of stress can negatively impact the body. Think about how your body reacts to stress. Do your shoulders tense up, does stress trigger a headache, or do you feel so overwhelmed that you can't focus? Whatever the case may be, if you experience prolonged periods of this, the effects will begin to take a toll on the body. Secondly, your relationships will flourish. The last benefit is that dealing with change lowers the risk of anxiety and depression. To help you navigate the change process, here are a few suggestions:

1. **Control what you can:** Think about the level of things that are within your control. If it helps, write down things that you can control and use them to help you begin to cope with the changes that are taking place.

2. **Attention to Self**: This is critical, especially after a loss. It does not matter what type of loss (loss of a relative, loss of a promotion, loss of a pet, or loss of a job). It is important for you to acknowledge what happened and, if applicable, what you learned from the incident. Some cases may even warrant seeking outside help.

3. **Thought Check**: Are you falling victim to negativity syndrome? Have you been thinking about the worst possible outcome? Have you been complaining more than usual? Be sure to think about how the change has affected your thinking, so that you can maintain a positive outlook.

4. **Live in the Present**: Take some time to enjoy life and the things that have not changed. Seeing the stability of other things in your life will also help to move you through the change continuum.

5. **What's on Your Schedule**: Whenever possible, prioritize scheduling routine things throughout the day. These things can include walking the dog, having coffee with a spouse, calling a friend every evening after work, or meeting a friend at the gym. When we spend time doing routine things, our mind takes a break. Think about it. How many times have you had the intention of stopping by the store on the way home only to get into the car and before you even realize it you are pulling into your driveway and don't even remember things you saw along the way? Driving is one of those routine tasks that we don't even have to think about. What other things do you do daily that fall into this category? Scheduling them periodically throughout the day will help you feel stable and contribute to your overall health and happiness.

6. **Give Yourself a Break**: Everyone goes through these stages, some faster than others. What is important is knowing how you react and working to ensure that you are acting proactively instead of reactively. The goal is to realize that change is inevitable and plan for it, instead of waiting until a change occurs and reacting negatively. Remember that the goal is to determine how you navigate the process, so that you can be sure you are equipped to assist students who will not be as resilient as you are when changes occur in their lives.

STOP & REFLECT

Now that we have discussed Emotional Intelligence and the stages of change, how does your EQ measure up? Answer yes or no to the following questions:

- **Recognizing Self:** Do you recognize situations in which your emotions may negatively impact situations?
- **Self-Management:** When you get upset, have you been willing to withhold your reactions until a more appropriate opportunity presents itself?
- **Social Intellect:** Does your perception of self-match how others perceive you?
- **Compassion for Others**: Are you able to predict how other people will react in certain situations?
- **Plotting Your Purpose**: Can you remain focused on goals even when your emotional state is heightened?

Use the area below to help you craft action steps to help strengthen any areas where your answer was "no."

Emotional Intelligence area to strengthen:

Action Steps: **Social Intellect**

1. journal
2. mirror moments
3.

Lastly, let's take a look at how you can apply this new knowledge to the classroom. To afford students the opportunity to reach the highest level of achievement, the adults in their lives must model how to choose peace. Peace is a choice for each of us. Learning to self-regulate our emotions and cope with change sets us on a path to focus on achieving purposeful goals. Educators can assist students by helping them attain these five aspects of emotional intelligence:

Step #1: *Enhance emotional vocabulary*: Many students begin school fully understanding the bare bones of emotions—happy, sad, mad, and scared. Just as we do with any other area, teachers should include time within the day for students to work on expanding their emotional vocabulary. Language is crucial to social-emotional competence and development. When children begin schooling, they embark on a journey that becomes more and more demanding and requires that they abstain from inappropriate behavior, conform to school-mandated rules, and perform targeted actions. Vocabulary development fosters the capacity to understand and abide by social requirements, deal with educational complexities, and interact constructively with educators and other children (Santiago-Poventud et al, 2015).

Before moving on to the second step of regulation, students' emotional vocabulary should be expanded to help them articulate their feelings. Articulation involves understanding what they are feeling, how their reactions affect themselves and other people, and the ability to convey thoughts and feelings appropriately in social settings.

Step #2: *Model self-regulation management:* Self-regulation denotes the mechanisms associated with the management of feelings, the ability to contemplate, and behavior. Children who grow up in literacy-rich settings usually develop reasoning, linguistic skills, metacognition, and self-regulation simultaneously due to using them to communicate during an array of purposes like classifying and signifying their feelings. In contrast, children in lower socioeconomic areas typically have limited language experiences and are likely to have smaller vocabularies and consequently have used language less frequently to direct their behavior or talk about what others may be thinking and feeling (Santiago-Poventud et al, 2015). Kaiser et al (2000) state that these students demonstrate a 40% deficiency in social skills and language usage and 20% express high-levels of inappropriate behavior that adversely impacts their ability to adjust to school. To make up for this delay, teachers should incorporate time within the school day for students to have conversations about their feelings and help students learn to scrutinize and modulate their feelings.

Step #3: *Working with others:* Collaboration is a critical part of the workplace. Employees spend between 50-80% of their time in collaborative tasks(Cross, Rebele, & Grant, 2016) . Think about the amount of time that you spend on the telephone, in meetings, replying to emails and then wondering at the end of the day why you weren't able to get the simplest independent task completed. More and more companies are moving to collective projects and using social apps and tools to help them increase productivity among employees (Cross, Rebele, & Grant, 2016). Due to this, it will become increasingly important for teachers to assist students in understanding how to work with others.

Step #4: *Respond with empathy:* Empathy allows us to serve as supportive members of a school and society. According to research conducted at the Harvard Graduate School of Education (2020), when children learn to empathize, they have higher academic success, are more engaged in class, converse better, are less aggressive, are able to form constructive relationships, and are less likely to bully other children. Empathy is a compassionate reaction to someone else's feelings. Children have the instinctive capability to have empathy, but it is not innate. It must be modeled, nurtured, and developed by the adults in their life. It is by watching us that students learn to attend to, care for, and understand how to sympathize for others. Time should be spent helping students develop this skill in the classroom.

Step #5: *Employ goal setting:* According to Schunk (1990), a goal is what a person is deliberately striving to achieve and goal setting involves the creation of a goal and revising it as needed. In addition, both goals and goal setting are contingent on a person's perceived self-efficacy. Self-efficacy is defined as the belief in your own competencies in terms of accomplishing a specified degree of efficiency (Bandura, 1986). Before having students begin to set goals, consider having conversations with them about their mindset and beliefs regarding their own capabilities. People are more likely to continue to work towards a goal if they believe they can achieve it. Goal setting is important because it helps students set a purpose for learning and behaving appropriately. It also serves as a reminder to help students stay focused on their purpose when considering the proper response in all situations.

STOP & REFLECT

Use the 6-step process in Appendix J (see also the image below) to help you shift your mindset regarding current personal or professional change you are currently working to adapt to.

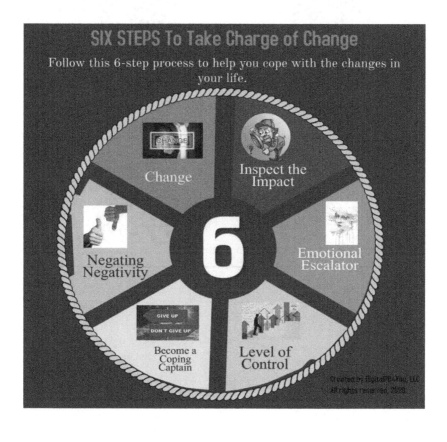

ADDITIONAL RESOURCES

Navigating Change:

Student Mindset Shifts for
Change:

Student Mindset Shifts
for Change:

EQ for Families:

DigitalPD4YOU.com

@JJJ8Z1

Educator Reflection Tip #21

How resilient are you during "change"?
How will you model resilience for students?

#BITESIZEPD

Strategy #1

Change- Why we must learn to cope!

Change, although inevitable, can be difficult because it can challenge, how we think, how we work, the quality of our relationships, our physical security, and even our sense of identity. Here are a few benefits to coping with change:

- It lowers the risk of anxiety and depression
- Your body feels healthier
- Your relationships will flourish
- By anticipating and embracing change, you will be able to help others learn to cope with change

---

#IMPROVEYOURSELF

Stages of the Change Process

There are four stages within the change process.

- Shock and Disorientation
- Anger and other emotional responses
- Coming to terms with the "new normal"
- Acceptance and moving forward

Old Way

New Way

Strategy #2

#ONTHEGOPD

Listen
Observe
Notice
Attend
...
...
Feel

Breathe
Pause
Invite
Allow
...
Greet

Strategy #3

Suggested Strategies to Cope with Change

Below is a list of suggested strategies to use to help cope with change.

- Determine your level of control
- Practice self-care after a loss
- Keep a pulse on your thought patterns
- Live in the Present
- Prioritize Scheduling Routines Daily
- Have a positive mindset regarding change

#PD4YOU

Adapting your process for the classroom

The following are just a few questions to consider when planning how to assist students with coping with change?

- How will you integrate this concept in your classroom? Will you spend time on it daily or as needed?
- If you have not allowed time to discuss this topic with students, has it had a negative impact on student behavior?
- What strategies will you teach students to help them cope with change?
- What process will students use to signal that they need assistance when changes take place in their lives?

Strategy #4

Other infographics are available for download at https://www.DigitalPD4you.com

Reflection Tip #22: How do you promote social and emotional wellness?

"Research has suggested that teacher-child relationships play a significant role in influencing young children's social and emotional development."

The Center on the Social Emotional Foundations for Early Learning

Social and emotional learning (SEL), involves the processes through which children and adults obtain and efficiently relate the information, approaches, and tactics needed to comprehend and cope with emotions, establish and attain constructive objectives, demonstrate and express empathy for others, create and sustain positive relationships, and hold themselves accountable for making responsible choices. These intrapersonal and interpersonal capabilities can be trained and assessed, and research indicates that students with these skills are more successful in academics and non-school related settings (National Research Council, 2009, 2012; Durlak, Weissberg, Dymnicki, Taylor, & Schellinger, 2011; Greenberg et al., 2001 as cited in Casel, 2012). There are many common terms for SEL. The most popular of these are 21st century skills, soft skills, noncognitive skills, and character education. Each description derives from a marginally different academic viewpoint and pulls upon a unique set of research, and each has its own associated areas and fields. For the purposes of this chapter, SEL or social and emotional learning will be used because it denotes learning and growth which corresponds with schools' underlying purpose of nurturing educational learning and developing functional citizens (Jones & Doolittle, 2017). An estimated $247 billion is spent every year on childhood mental health disorders. Research conducted by Weare and Nind (2011) report that about 25% of children and adolescents have a recognizable mental health problem. Of those, the Center for Disease Control and Prevention (2013) says 1 in 5 have met the documented benchmarks for a mental health disorder.

The Center for Disease Control and Prevention (CDC) defines childhood mental disorder as "mental conditions that can be detected and initiated in childhood which cause significant variations in the way children naturally learn, perform, or manage emotions." Common examples of mental disorders include behavior disorders, mood and anxiety disorders, attention-deficit/hyperactivity disorder (ADHD), Tourette syndrome, and autism spectrum disorders. Mental health is a key factor in general health.

Children who have mental health problems and disorders often have difficulties at home, in school, and any setting that involves forming relationships. These impediments can also inhibit healthy development overall. Schools have the unique opportunity to provide students with tools to help foster positive mental health and build resilience. Schools can also offer children strategies to increase the likelihood that they will flourish in difficult situations and are able to maintain and endure when they encounter negative stresses throughout life. When children have less than favorable home environments, intervention provided by the school can serve as the bridge that helps them persevere and continue on a positive life trajectory (Gross, 2008). It is evident that in order to lessen levels of childhood mental illness, interventions and supports should be put in place early in life. Targeted supports work best when instituted prior to the onset of significant symptoms of mental health disorders. Prevention can also assist with endeavors to expand outreach to children who are unable to access the treatment or who receive improper services (Knitzer, 1985; Tuma, 1989 as cited in Greenberg, Domitrovich, & Bumbarger, 2001). Researchers have suggested that educators should begin adopting a public health methodology by implementing SEL programs to help reduce the effects both in and outside of school settings. Ultimately, the aim of public health is to enhance the overall population's welfare which entails averting viruses, syndromes, injuries, and other problem behaviors while supporting actions that improve health and wellness. The most successful schools prepare students not only to excel on tests in the school environment, but also to excel in the tests of life. Schools are realizing that social emotional competence and educational achievement are intertwined and both must be prioritized. Synchronized instruction in both areas boosts students' capacity to achieve not only in school, but in life. (Zins & Elias, 2007).

STOP & REFLECT

Before we continue, consider the social and emotional skills students need to be productive citizens in the world. List the top five things that you believe influence students' ability to develop these skills:

1. _____

2. _____

3. _____

4. _____

5. _____

Most educators understand the need to integrate social and emotional skills into instruction but are unsure of exactly what should be included and how to incorporate them. Wang, Haertel, and Walberg (1997) conducted research to determine the characteristics that promote resilience in learning for students who are at risk of educational failure. The authors found that nine out of the top ten most influential categories for healthy promotion and primary prevention occur within classrooms and during school-wide practices.

Let's take a look at the implications of each of the influences on social emotional learning and the academic development of children (Wang, et al, 1997):

#1: Managing the Classroom: Classroom culture is the most important influence on students' academic and social success. Educators should clearly establish behavioral and academic expectations, communicate the level of success that students should strive to attain, and explicitly define the cultural norms of the classroom.

#2: Home Environment/Parent Support: When teachers cultivate a partnership with their parents, children are more passionate about school, have fervent attitudes about learning, attain higher marks, and are more apt to enroll in college or career-ready opportunities (Henderson & Mapp, 2002 as cited in Fowler-White, 2020). When students feel that their parents are involved and concerned about their academic success, they tend to work harder and choose more complex tasks.

#3: Teacher-Student Relationships: Educators show genuine concern for their students, work to develop sustainable relationships with students, and understand the importance of providing students time to work independently with support. Each of these has been proven to decrease student stress and diminish the probability of academic failure. Teachers should serve as academic leaders, and also as trusted and positive role models for students.

#4: Student-Student Associations: To help build a sense of community, teachers must facilitate positive interactions among students. This action must be intentional, grounded in clear and consistent classroom rules, and foster respect for diverse learning styles, cultures, and the unique qualities of all students.

#5: Instructional Value: Students are more successful and show more academic achievement in classrooms where the teacher has high expectations, implements stimulating and rigorous curriculum, provides multiple pathways for students to access grade-level content, and allows students to productively struggle. This teaches them the benefit of productive struggle and how to persevere through challenges.

#6: School Climate: The overall school climate should motivate students to strive for academic excellence. School leaders should work to create an environment that emphasizes students' academic accomplishments, spotlights them publicly, provides incentives, stresses community, and establishes connectivity and belonging at school. They should also establish programs designed to respond when students feel disconnected to the school.

#7: Classroom Atmosphere: Teachers should work to create an environment in which students are expected to persist in their schoolwork and achieve at high levels academically. Student experiences, culture, and academic needs should be infused into instruction to keep them engaged and reduce learning gaps.

#8: Teaching in the Classroom: Students achieve the most success when teachers have well-planned lessons, involve students in making educational decisions, customize and personalize lessons to meet the academic needs of individual learners, and work to maximize instructional time.

#9: Educational Collaborations: High student engagement, incorporating goal setting, and providing ample opportunities for students to participate in cooperative groups have also been proven to positively influence student outcomes and attitudes outside of school.

#10: Measuring Learning: Teachers who understand the role that assessment plays in the teaching and learning process intentionally work to create a data-driven instructional cycle. These cycles include a feedback loop where students set academic and behavior goals, staying focused on the criteria they must master to accomplish the goals they have set. The cycles also include personalized check-ins with students to determine scaffolds and provide next steps, self-progress monitoring by students as it relates to their goals, and ongoing monitoring and support on the part of the teacher.

Effective learning evolves after caring connections have been formed and when programs are intellectually stimulating, appealing, and meaningful for students. Social and emotional skills should be incorporated both inside and outside of school settings. Hawkins, Smith, and Catalano (2004) contend that, when implemented effectively, SEL curriculum and instructional strategies can help to avert or thwart involvement in hazardous behaviors such as drug-use, violence, and bullying, along with reducing the likelihood of students choosing to drop out of school. Bond and Hauf (2004) contend that for wellness programs to be sustainable and successful, it is crucial to include a continuous process which encompasses a well-designed system to track progress, assess effectiveness, and adapt implementation.

The Collaborative for Academic, Social, and Emotional Learning (CASEL) states that successful social and emotional wellness programs should begin in prekindergarten and continue throughout high schooling for all children (2003). CASEL has identified five interconnected types of mental, emotional, and behavior-based competencies to be included in SEL programming. These five capability bands are described below:

1. **Cognizance of Self:** This band revolves around the learners ability to correctly identify one's feelings and beliefs and their impact on actions. Children who have grasped this competency should be able

to precisely evaluate their strengths and weaknesses as well as exhibit an accurate perception of self-confidence and hopefulness.

2. **Regulation of Self**: This capacity band requires children to master the ability to manage their feelings, beliefs, and actions efficiently in a variety of situations. Within this band, children should learn to cope with stress, manage impulses, receive training on self-motivation, and be taught to endure while working on individual and educational goals they have set for themselves.

3. **Civil Consciousness:** In this band, children take the viewpoint of and sympathize with others from varied environments and cultures to understand societal and virtuous measures for behavior, and to acknowledge family, school, and community supplies and services.

4. **The Architecture of Bonding**: This capacity band focuses on a youth's aptitude to begin and sustain strong and gratifying connections with different individuals and groups. This includes speaking clearly, listening attentively, collaborating, holding out against improper societal constraints, dealing with disputes productively, and requesting and extending assistance when necessary.

5. **Action Accountability**: Lastly, this band highlights the importance of students' ability to make productive decisions and take accountability for their actions by making ethically appropriate decisions related to the well-being of others and societal norms, while rationally considering the effects of their behavior.

STOP & REFLECT

Now that we have learned about the five core aptitudes that the Collaborative for Academic, Social, and Emotional Learning (Casel) outlines for successful implementation of SEL curriculums, think about the SEL program that your school is implementing. Categorize your current practices using the chart in Appendix K to determine if there are areas within your current program that need to be strengthened. Determine if they meet the expectations of the competencies and whether your school is setting the stage for students' academic and behavioral success.

ADDITIONAL RESOURCES

Social and Emotional
Learning (ASCD PD
Resources):

Social and Emotional
Learning: Tools from NBCT
Educators:

*CASEL'S Curated List of SEL
in Action (Video Library):*

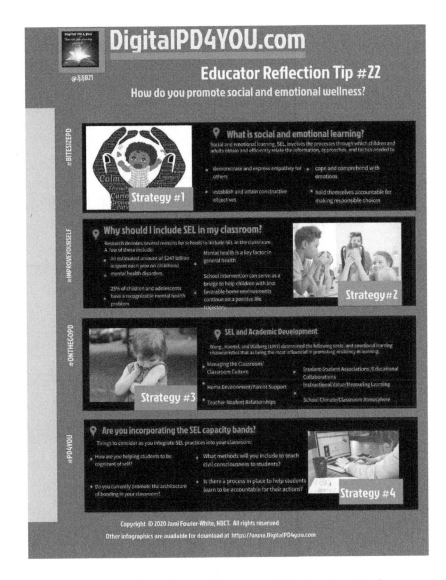

Infographics for each Reflection Tip are available for download at www. DigitalPD4You.com

Appendices

Appendix A:
Seeking Self-Reflection

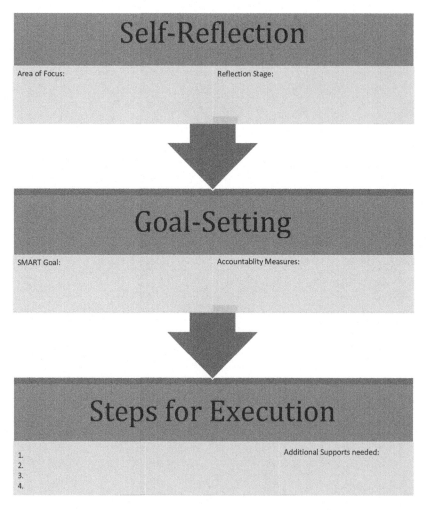

Self-Reflection

Area of Focus: Reflection Stage:

Goal-Setting

SMART Goal: Accountablity Measures:

Steps for Execution

1.   Additional Supports needed:
2.
3.
4.

©Jami Fowler-White, 2020; Educator Reflection Tips, Volume #2

Appendix B:
Creating a Growth Mindset Culture

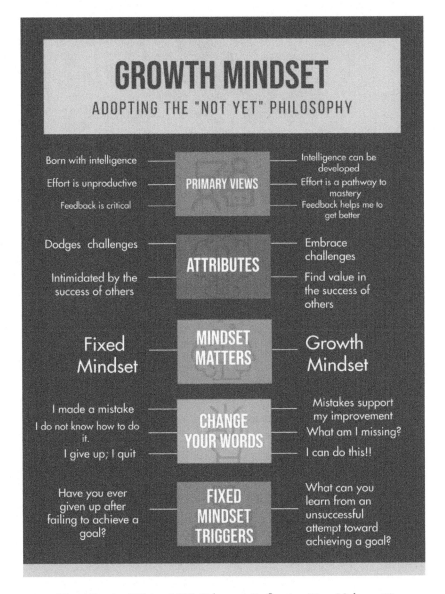

©Jami Fowler-White, 2020; Educator Reflection Tips, Volume #2

Appendix C:
Focusing on the Reader

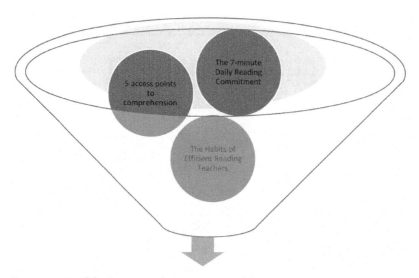

Part #1: Highlight or circle your area of focus:

1. Access Point to for Comprehending Complex Texts
2. The Seven-Minute Daily Reading Commitment
3. Gauging student needs
4. The Instructional Toolbox
5. Explicit Modeling
6. Building a Print-Rich Atmosphere
7. Family and Community Engagement
8. The Brain and Reading

Part #2: Action Steps to improve reading instruction in _____.

A.

B.

C.

Appendix D:
Acclimatize Your Online Classroom

In the space below, outline your plan to help students develop independence in these vital areas to increase student success in the online areas.

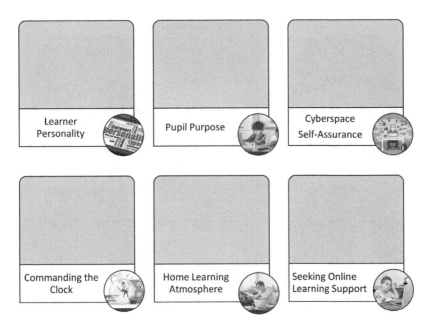

Learner Personality

Pupil Purpose

Cyberspace Self-Assurance

Commanding the Clock

Home Learning Atmosphere

Seeking Online Learning Support

©Jami Fowler-White, 2020; Educator Reflection Tips, Volume #2

Appendix E:
Digital Citizenship Framework

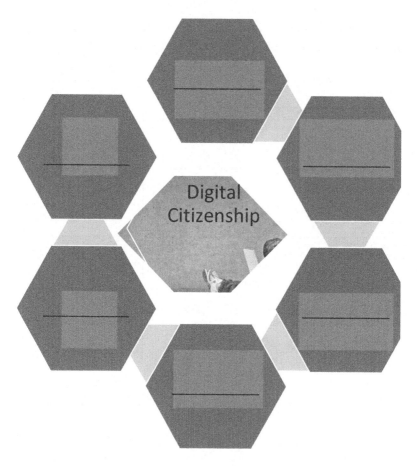

©Jami Fowler-White, 2020; Educator Reflection Tips, Volume #2

Appendix F:
Web 2.0 Glossary

Suggested digital tools for schools and teachers to begin with when determining which Web 2.0 tools to integrate into their instruction. When choosing tools, educators should first consider the intent of the standard and then select digital resources which will help to strengthen instruction and/or assist students with demonstrating mastery of the standard.

Screencasting Tools

- Educreations Interactive Whiteboard (IOS App)
- Explain Everything (IOS App)
- Lensoo Create (Android App)
- Loom
- Nimbus Capture
- Show Me (IOS app)
- Screencastify
- Screencast-O-Matic

Podcasting and Creating Videos:

- Buzzsprout
- Canvas
- Express Scribe
- Loopster
- MailChimp
- Podomatic
- WeVideo

Presentations:

- EdCanvas
- CuePrompter
- Crocodoc
- Insert Learning

Student Engagement Tools:

- Bamboozle
- BaseCamp
- Bubbl.us
- Chart It
- Draw.io.
- Edublogs
- Fablement
- FlipGrid
- Funapero
- Involve.me
- Mindomo
- Narakeet
- Netstory
- Once
- Padlet
- Prezi
- Reverb Record
- Stringflix
- TagX
- Thingslink

Appendix G:
Virtual Learning - Using the Essential Elements

Part #1: As you begin, take note of the core ideas from each of the learning theories that best align with your instructional practices.

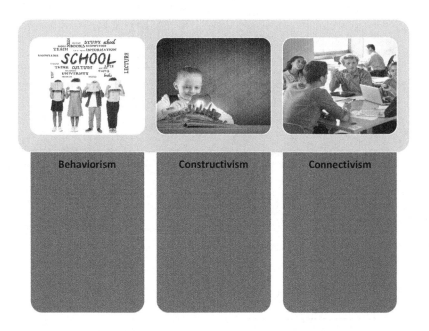

Behaviorism   Constructivism   Connectivism

Part #2: Now that you have read through all the learning theories, write down three practices/principles that you are committing to incorporating into your instructional practices:

1.
2.
3.

©Jami Fowler-White, 2020; Educator Reflection Tips, Volume #2

Appendix H:
Solidifying Student Engagement

Which characteristic(s) of societal atmosphere will you work to improve?

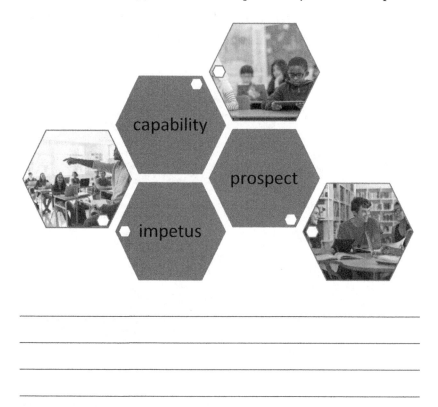

_____

_____

_____

_____

Write action steps to help guide you as you create engagement that positively impact students ability to learn:

	What will you do to create a societal atmosphere in your classroom?	Timeline for Implementation
Attainment Mindset		
Unwavering Support		
Purposeful Objective		
E.M.P.O.W.E.R. Feedback		
Collaborative Community		

©Jami Fowler-White, 2020; Educator Reflection Tips, Volume #2

Appendix I:
Cultivating Cultural Competence

Think about your classroom. List culturally responsive practices that you are currently using. After creating your list, categorize your practices under each of the four elements provided in the figure below. Analyze the final categories to determine an element that you will work to strengthen. Use a different color pen to add 2-3 strategies you will commit to integrating under the category you will work to strengthen.

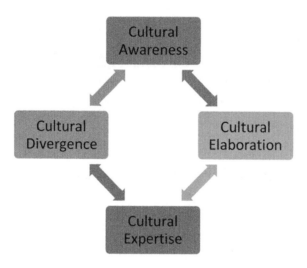

Adapted from Geneva Gray's 2002 article,
Preparing for Culturally Responsive Teaching.

Cultural Awareness	Cultural Elaboration	Cultural Expertise	Cultural Divergence

©Jami Fowler-White, 2020; Educator Reflection Tips, Volume #2

Appendix J:
Taking Charge of Change

Use the template below to measure how you are coping with the changes that are currently occurring in your personal and professional life.

Chronicle the Change Describe your current situation	
Inspect the Impact How is the change affected your life?	
Emotional Escalator What emotions have you been feeling regarding the change?	
Level of Control Is there anything that you can do to fix your current situation?	
Become a Coping Captain What is your strategy to cope with the change?	
Negating Negativity What positive aspects can you choose to focus on?	

©Jami Fowler-White, 2020; Educator Reflection Tips, Volume #2

Appendix K:
Social and Emotional Learning-Measuring the Likelihood of Success

How do your school/classroom SEL strategies measure up? Use the characteristics outlined in Reflection Tip #22 to help you outline current practices that meet the expectation for each of the social and emotional learning competencies. List five of your current SEL practices for each of the research-based capacities.

SEL Aptitudes	Practice #1	Practice #2	Practice #3	Practice #4	Practice #5
Cognizance of Self					
Regulation of Self					
Civil Consciousness					
The Architecture of Bonding					
Action Accountability					

©Jami Fowler-White, 2020; Educator Reflection Tips, Volume #2

References

Aguilar, E. (2015). Making connections: Culturally Responsive Teaching and the Brain. *Edutopia*

Ahmed, S. & Rosen, L. (2019). A growth mindset: Essential for student and faculty success. *Philosophy of Teaching.* Retrieved from https://www.facultyfocus.com/articles/philosophy-of-teaching/a-growth-mindset-essential-for-student-and-faculty-success/ on October 9, 2020.

ASCD (2017). What exactly is depth of knowledge? (Hint: It's not a wheel!) *Inservice*, Association for Supervision and Curriculum Development.

Aupperle, R. L., Melrose, A. J., Stein, M. B., & Paulus, M. P. (2012). Executive function and PTSD: Disengaging from trauma. Neuropharmacology, 62(2), 686–694.

Baleghizadeh, S. & Naeim, M.Y. (2011). *Journal of Theory in Education and Practice.* 7 (1): 111-123. Retrieved from https://dergipark.org.tr/tr/download/article-file/63235 on July 13, 2020.

Bandura, A. (In press). An agentic perspective on positive psychology. In S. J. Lopez (Ed.). Positive psychology: Expecting the best in people (Vol. 1). New York: Praeger.

Bandura, A., & Cervone, D. (1983). Self-evaluative and self-efficacy mechanisms governing the motivational effects of goal systems. Journal of Personality and Social Psychology, 45, 1017-1028.

Bartolome, L. (1994). Beyond the methods fetish: Toward a humanizing pedagogy. Harvard Educational Review, 64, 173-194.

Baumann, J. F., Kame'enui, E. J., & Ash, G. E. (2003). Research on vocabulary instruction: Voltaire redux. In J. Flood, D. Lapp, J. R. Squire, & J. M. Jensen (Eds.), *Handbook of Research on Teaching the English Language Arts,* 2nd ed, 752-785.

Beachum, F. & McCray, C. (2008). Dealing with cultural collision in urban schools: What pre-service educators should know. In G. Goodman, Education psychology: An application of critical constructivism, p. 53-70. New York: Lang.

Becker, S. A, Cummins, M., Davis, A. Freeman, A., Glesinger Hall, C. & Ananthanarayanan, V. (2017). NMC Horizon Report: 2017 Higher Education Edition. Austin, TX: The New Media Consortium.

Blackburn, B. (2000). Using gradual release in remote learning. Retrieved on November 25, 2020 from https://www.middleweb.com/44162using-gradual-release-in-remote-learning/

Bloom, B. S. (1956). Taxonomy of educational objectives handbook: Cognitive domains. New York: David McKay.

Boholano, H. (2017). Smart social networking: 21st century teaching and learning skills. *Research in Pedagogy,* 7(1), 21-29.

Boulware-Gooden, R., Carreker, S., Thornhill, A., & Joshi, R. (2007, September) Instruction of metacognitive strategies enhances reading comprehension and vocabulary achievement of third-grade students: the use of metacognitive strategies helps students to 'think about their thinking' before, during, and after they read. *The Reading Teacher,* 61(1), 70-78.

Boyles, N. (2004). Constructing meaning through kid-friendly comprehension strategy instruction. Florida: Maupin House.

Bransford, J., Brown, A., & Cocking, R. (1999). How people learn: Brain, mind experience and school. Washington, D.C.: National Academy Press/National Research Council.

Breiseth, L., Garcia, S., & Butler, S. (2020). Culturally responsive teaching: What you need to know. Retrieved on 11/11/2020 from https://www.understood.org/en/school-learning/for-educators/universal-design-for-learning/what-is-culturally-responsive-teaching

Brennan, D. & Hiebert, E. (2010). The impact of professional development on students' opportunity to read. In E. Hiebert & D. Reutzel (Eds.). Revisiting Silent Reading: New directions for teachers and researchers. Newark, DE: International Reading Association.

Bridges, W. & Bridges, S. (1980). Transitions: making sense of life's changes. Boston, MA: Da Capo Life Long Books.

Brock, F. J., Thomsen, W. E., & Kohl, J. P. (1992). The effects of demographics on computer literacy of university freshmen. Journal of Research on Computing in Education, 24(4), 563-570.

Brophy, J. & Good, T. (1986). Teacher behavior and student achievement. In M. Wittrock, *Handbook of Research on Teaching.* 3: 328-375.

Brown-Jeffy, S. & Cooper, J. (2011). Toward a conceptual framework of culturally relevant pedagogy: An overview of the conceptual and theorical literature. *Teacher Education Quarterly.* 65-84.

Canter, L. & Canter, M. (1994). The High-Performing Teacher: Avoiding burnout and increasing your motivation. Santa Monica, CA: Lee Canter & Associates.

Catania, A. & Laties, V. (1999). Pavlov and Skinner: Two lives in science (An introduction of B.f. Skinner's some responses to the stimulus "Pavlov". *Journal of the experimental analysis of behavior.* 72 (3): 455-461.

Caviness, S. (2020). The relationship between at-home reading literacy scores of beginning kindergarteners. (Doctoral Dissertation). Walden University

Cherry, K. (2020). 5 components of Emotional Intelligence. Retrieved on 10/31/2020 from https://www.verywellmind.com/components-of-emotional-intelligence-2795438.

College Star. Using web 2.0 tools to engage learners. Retrieved on 10/24/2020 from https://www.collegestar.org/modules/using-web-2-0-tools-to-engage-learners

Coomey, M., & Stephenson, J. (2001). Online learning: It is all about dialogue, involvement, support and control – According to the research. In J. Stephenson (Ed.), Teaching and learning online: Pedagogies for new technologies (pp. 37–52). London: Kogan Page.

Cooper. P. (2003). Effective white teachers of black children: Teaching within a community. *Journal of Teacher Education.* 54: 413-427.

Costa, A. & Kallick, B. (2015). Five strategies for questioning with intention. *Questioning for Learning.* 73 (1): 66-69.

Cross, R., Rebele, R., & Grant, A. (2016). Collaborative Overload. *Harvard Business Journal.* Retrieved on November 7, 2020 from https://hbr.org/2016/01/collaborative-overload.

Cunningham-Morris, A. (2016). The Principal Influence: A framework for developing capacity for principals. Alexandria, VA: ASCD.

Curtain, M. (2017). Bill Gates this is the 'safest' age to give a child a smartphone. Retrieved on July 28, 2020 from https://www.inc.com/melanie-curtin/bill-gates-says-this-is-the-safest-age-to-give-a-child-a-smartphone.html

David, S. (2015). Emotional agility: Get unstuck, embrace change, and thrive in work and life. New York, NY: Penguin Random House, LLC.

Delpit, L. (1995). Otiier people's children: Cultural conflict in the classroom. New York: New Press.

Dewey, J. (1933). *How We Think.* New York: D. C. Heath. Classic and highly influential discussion of thinking.

DiClemente, C. & Fava, J. (1988). Measuring processes of change: Applications to the cessation of smoking. *Journal of Consulting and Clinical Psychology.* 56(4): 520-528.

Dimitriadis, M. (2015). 10 growth mindset questions to ask students. Retrieved on October 1, 202 from https://www.makersempire.com/category/growth-mindset/

Dixon, M. (2010). Creating effective student engagement in online courses: What do students find engaging? *Journal of the Scholarship of Teaching and Learning.* 10(2): 1-13.

Duke, N., Pearson, D., Strachan, S., & Billman, A. (2011). Essential elements of fostering and teaching reading comprehension. In J. Samuels, and Farstrup, A. (Eds). What research says about reading instruction. Fourth Edition. Newark, DE: International Reading Association.

Durlak, J. A., Weissberg, R. P., Dymnicki, A. B., Taylor, R. D., & Schellinger, K. (2011). The impact of enhancing students' social and emotional learning: A meta-analysis of school-based universal interventions. Child Development, 82, 405-432.

Fernando, S. & Marikar, F. (2017). Constructivist teaching/learning theory and participatory teaching methods. *Journal of Curriculum and Teaching. 6(1): 110-122.*

Fisher, D. & Frey, N. (2020). Show & tell: A video column/direct instruction in Early Reading. *Educational Leadership.* 78(3): 76-77.

For Educators: How to build empathy and strengthen your school community. Retrieved on 11/8/2020 from https://mcc.gse.harvard.edu/resources-for-educators/how-build-empathy-strengthen-school-community.

Fordham, S., & Ogbu, J. (1986). Black students' success: Coping with the burden of "acting White." Urban Review, 18, 1-31.

Fowler-White, J. (2020). Educator reflection tips: How often do you reflect on your practice. Memphis, TN: Digital PD 4 You.

Fulwiler, T. (1987). Teaching with writing. Portsmouth, N.H.: Boynton/Cook.

Gagné, R. M. (1977). The conditions of learning. New York: Holt, Rinehart & Winston.

Gay, G. (2000). Culturally responsive teaching: Theory, research, and practice. New York: Teachers College Press.

Gay, G. (2002). Preparing for Culturally responsive teaching. *Journal of Teacher Education.* 53(2): 106-116.

Gibson, C. C. (1998). The distance learner's academic self-concept. In C. C. Gibson (Ed.) Distance learners in higher education: institutional responses for quality outcomes (p. 65-76). Madison, WI.: Atwood Publishing.

Gore, W. (2002). Navigating change: A field guide to personal growth. Memphis, TN: Team Trek.

Graham, C., Henrie, C., & Gibbons, A. (2013). Developing models and theory for blended learning research. In A. G. Picciano, C. D. Dziuban, & C. R. Graham (Eds.), Blended learning: Research perspectives, volume 2. New York, NY: Routledge.

Grant, P. & Basye, D. (2014). Personalized Learning: A guide for engaging students with technology. Washington, DC: International Society for Technology in Education

Graham, S., Bruch, J., Fitzgerald, J., Friedrich, L., Furgeson, J., Greene, K., Kim, J., Lyskawa, J., Olson, C.B., & Smither Wulsin, C. (2016). Teaching secondary students to write effectively (NCEE 2017-4002). Washington, DC: National Center for Education Evaluation and Regional Assistance (NCEE), Institute of Education Sciences, U.S. Department of Education. Retrieved from the NCEE website: http://whatworks.ed.gov.

Graves, M. & Fitzgerald, J. (2003). Scaffolding reading experiences for multilingual classrooms. In English learners: Reaching the highest level of English literacy by G. Garcia (Ed). Newark, DE: International Reading Association. 96-124.

Grayson, R. (n.d.). Emotional Intelligence: A Summary. Retrieved on 2013 from http://www.visionrealization.com

Greenwald, A. G., & Krieger, L. H. (2006). Implicit bias: Scientific foundations. *California Law Review, 94*(4), 945-967.

Gu, X., Zhu, Y. & Guo, X (2013). Meeting the "Digital Natives": Understanding the Acceptance of Technology in Classrooms. Educational Technology & Society, 16 (1), 392–402.

Guo, R., Dobson, S, Petrina, S. (2008). Digital natives, digital immigrants: An analysis of age and ICT competency in teacher education. *J. Educational Computing Research.* Vol 38 (3): 235-254.

Hale-Benson, J. (1986). Black children: Their roots, culture, and learning styles (Rev. ed.). Baltimore: The Johns Hopkins University Press.

Hall, P. Simeral, A. (2010) Building Teachers' Capacity for Success: A collaborative approach for coaches and school leaders. Virginia, Alexandria ,VA: ASCD

Hart, B. & Risley, T. (2003). The early catastrophe: The 30 million word gap by age 3. *American Educator. 4-9.*

Hattie, J. (2008). *Visible Learning: A Synthesis of Over 800 Meta-Analyses Relating to Achievement,* Routledge.

Hattie, J. (2012). Visible Learning for Teachers: Maximizing Impact on Learning. New York, NY: Routledge.

Healy, J. (1990). Endangered minds: Why children don't think and what can be done about it. New York: Touchstone.

Henderson, A. T., & Berla, N. (1994). A New Generation of Evidence: The Family is Critical to Student Achievement. National Committee for Citizens in Education, Columbia, MD.

Hess, K. (2013). "A Guide for Using Webb's Depth of Knowledge with Common Core State Standards". Common Core Institute, 2013. Retrieved on December 21, 2020 from https://education.ohio.gov/getattachment/Topics/Teaching/Educator-Evaluation-System/How-to-Design-and-Select-Quality-Assessments/Webbs-DOK-Flip-Chart.pdf.aspx

Holmberg, B. (1995). Theory and practice of distance education. London: Routledge.

Hordsford, S., Grosland, T, Morgan Gunn, K. (2011). Pedagogy of the personal and professional: Toward a framework for culturally relevant leadership. *Journal of School Leadership.* 21: 582-606.

Hu, S. and Kuh, G. (2001). Being (dis)engaged in educationally purposeful activities: the influences of student and institutional characteristics. Paper presented at the American Educational Research Association Annual Conference, Seattle, WA, 10 - 14 April.

Hussar, B., Zhang, J., Hein, S., Wang, K., Roberts, A., Cui, J., Smith, M., Bullock Mann, F., Barmer, A., & Dilig, R. (2020). The Condition of Education 2020 (NCES 2020-144). U.S. Department of Education. Washington, DC: National Center for Education Statistics. Retrieved July 11, 2020 from https://nces.ed.gov/pubsearch/pubsinfo.asp?pubid=2020144

Illie, M. & Cocorada, S. (2014). Interactions of students' personality in the online learning environment. *Procedia Social and Behavioral Sciences.* 128: 117-122.

Isaacson, W. (2014). The innovators: how a group of hackers, geniuses, and geeks created the digital revolution. New York: NY: Simon & Schuster.

ISTE Standards: New Digital Citizenship. *Iste.org.* N.p., 2018. Web. 12 Oct. 2018.

Johnson, L. (2007). Rethinking successful school leadership in challenging U.S. schools: Culturally responsive practices in school-community relationships. *International Studies in Educational Administration. 35(3): 49- 57.*

Johnson, S. (2005). Your Brain on Video Games: Could they actually be good for you? *Discover, 39-43.* Retrieved from http://www2.centralcatholichs.com/copied%20articles%20to%20review/Neuro/video%20games%20and%20brain.PDF

Johnson, S. (2005) Everything Bad is Good for You: how today's popular culture is actually making us smarter. New York: Riverhead Books.

Jones, S. (1999). Multisensory vocabulary instruction: Guidelines and activities. Retrieved July 11, 2020, from The Reading Rockets website: https://www.readingrockets.org/article/multisensory-vocabulary-instruction-guidelines-and-activities.

Jung, I. (2001). Building a theoretical framework of web-based instruction in the context of distance education. British Journal of Educational Technology, 32(5), 525 – 534.

Karsten, M. C., & Roth, R. M. (1998). The relationship of computer experience and computer self-efficacy to performance in introductory computer literacy courses. Journal of Research on Computing in Education, 31(1), 14-24.

Katsev, I. (2013). Cognoscere. In different Language. Retrieved on December 19, 2020 from Cognoscere in English. Cognoscere Meaning and Latin to English Translation (indifferentlanguages.com).

Kehrwald, B. (2008). Understanding social presence in text-based online learning environments. Distance Education, 29(1), 89-106.

Kift, S. & Nelson, K. (2005) Beyond curriculum reform: Embedding the transition experience, in Higher education in a changing world, Proceedings of the 28th HERDSA Annual Conference, Sydney, 3-6, July 2005.

King, J. (1994). The burden of acting White re-examined: Towards a critical genealogy of acting Black. Paper presented at the annual meeting of the American Educational Research Association, New Orleans. As cited in Ladson-Billings, G. (1995). But that's just good teaching! The case for culturally relevant pedagogy. Theory into Practice. 34(3): 159-165.

Kolb, D. (1984). Experiential Learning. Englewood Cliffs, New Jersey: Prentice Hall.

Krause, K. and Coates, H. (2008). Student engagement in first-year university. Assessment and Evaluation in Higher Education, 33(5), 493- 505.

Kuh, G.D., Kinzie, J., Buckley, J.A., Bridges, B.K. & Hayek, J. C. (2007). Piecing together the student success Puzzle research, propositions and recommendations *ASHE Higher Education Report Series,* 32(5). San Francisco: Jossey-Bass.

Kuhn, M. & Schwanenflugel, P. (2009). Time, engagement, and support: Lessons from a four-year fluency intervention. In E. Hiebert (ed). Reading More, Reading Better. New York: Guilford Press: 141-160.

Ladson-Billings, G. (1994). The dreamkeepers: Successful teaching for African-American students. San Francisco: Jossey-Bass.

Ladson-Billings, G. (1995). But that's just good teaching! The case for culturally relevant pedagogy. Theory into Practice. 34(3): 159-165.

Lynch, R. & Dembo, M. (2004). The relationship between self-regulation and online learning in a blended learning context. *International Review of Research in Open and Distance Learning. 5(2): 1-14.*

Majors, R., & Billson, J. (1992). Cool pose: The dilemmas of Black manhood in America. New York: Lexington Books.

Marzano, R., Pickering, D., & Pollock, J. (2001). Classroom instruction that works: Research-based strategies for increasing student achievement. Alexandria, VA: ASCD.

McCoog, I. (2008). 21st Century teaching and learning. Education Resource Center. Retrieved 90 10/24/2020 from eric.ed.gov/PDFS/ED502607.pdf.

Mezirow J. 1991. Transformative dimensions of adult learning. San Francisco, CA: Jossey Bass.

Miner, H. R., FV. (2007). Race, narrative inquiry, and self-study in curriculum and teacher education. Education and Urban Society, 39(4), 584-609.

Mizzel, H. (2010). Why professional development matters. Ohio: Learning Forward.

Mohamad, M. & Jais, J. (2016). Emotional intelligence and job performance: A study among Malaysian Teachers. *Procedia Economics and Finance*. 35: 674-682.

Morin, A. (2020). How to increase your social intelligence. *Very Well Mind*. Retrieved on October 31, 2020 from https://www.verywellmind.com/what-is-social-intelligence-4163839.

Muhammad, G. (2020). Cultivating Genius: An equity framework for culturally and historically responsive literacy. New York: Scholastic.

Murray, D. (1985). A Writer Teaches Writing, 2nd Edition. Chicago: Houghton Mifflin Harcourt.

National Center for Education Statistics. (2017). *National Assessment of Educational Progress: An overview of NAEP*. Washington, D.C.: National Center for Education Statistics, Institute of Education Sciences, U.S. Dept. of Education.

National Center for Education Statistics. (2019). *National Assessment of Educational Progress: An overview of NAEP*. Washington, D.C.: National Center for Education Statistics, Institute of Education Sciences, U.S. Dept. of Education.

National Commission on Writing (2003). The need for a writing revolution. The neglected "R". New York: College Entrance Examination Board.

National Council for Teachers of Mathematics (2014). Principles to actions: ensuring mathematical success for all. Reston, VA: NCTM, National Council of Teachers of Mathematics

Ngussa, B. (2017). Gagne's nine events of instruction in teaching-learning transaction: Evaluation of teachers by high school students in Musoma-Tanzania. *International Journal of Education and Research*. 2(7): 189-206.

Nichols, M. (2007). Comprehension through conversation: The power of purposeful talk in the Reading Workshop. Portsmouth, NH: Heinemann.

November, A. (2001) Empowering Students with Technology. Thousand Oaks, CA: Corwin Press.

Osguthorpe, R.T. & Graham, C.R. (2003). Blended Learning Environments: Definitions and Directions. *Quarterly Review of Distance Education, 4*(3), 227. Retrieved July 12, 2020 from https://www.learntechlib.org/p/97576/.

Palloff, R. M., and Pratt, K. (1999). Building Learning Communities in Cyberspace: Effective strategies for the online classroom. San Francisco: Jossey-Bass.

Paris S., Byrnes J. (1989) The Constructivist Approach to Self-Regulation and Learning in the Classroom. In: Zimmerman B.J., Schunk D.H. (eds) Self-Regulated Learning and Academic Achievement. Springer Series in Cognitive Development. Springer, New York, NY. https://doi.org/10.1007/978-1-4612-3618-4_7

Parsons, Seth & Richey, Leila & Parsons, Allison. (2014). Student learning: Engagement & motivation. Phi Delta Kappan. 95. 23-27.

Peters, O. (1998). Learning and Teaching in Distance Education: Analyses and interpretations from an international perspective. London: Kogan Page.

Pewewardy, C. (1993). Culturally responsible pedagogy in action: An American Indian magnet school. In E. Hollins, J. King, & W. Hayman (Eds.), Teaching diverse populations: Formulating a knowledge base (pp. 77-92). Albany: State University of New York Press.

Phipps, R., & Merisotis, J. (1999). What's the difference: A review of contemporary research on the effectiveness of distance learning in higher education. Washington, DC: The Institute for Higher Education Policy.

Pollock, J., Ford, S., & Black, M. (2012). Minding the achievement gap: one class at a time. Alexandria, Va.: ASCD, 2012

Prenksy, M. (2001). Digital natives, digital immigrants. On the Horizon, 9(5), 1–6.

Richardson, J., & Lewis, E. (2018). Next step forward in reading intervention: The RISE framework. New York: Scholastic.

Riegel, C. & Mete, R. (2018). Educational technologies for K-12 learners: What digital natives and digital immigrants can teach one another. *Educational Planning*. 24(4), 49-58.

Ribble, M. (2015). Digital citizenship in schools: nine elements all students should know. United States of America: International Society for Technology in Education.

Roblyer, M. D. (1999). Is Choice Important in Distance Learning? A study of student motives for taking Internet-based courses at the high school and community college levels. Journal of Research on Computing Education, 32(1), 157 – 171.

Rosenshine, B. (2008). Five meanings of direct instruction. Center for Innovation and Improvement.

Santiago-Poventud, L, Corbett, N., Daunic, A., Aydin, B., Lane, H., & Smith, S. (2015). Developing social-emotional vocabulary to support self-regulation for young children at risk for emotional and behavioral problems. *International Journal of School and Cognitive Psychology*. 2 (3): 1000143

Sheninger, E. (2014). Digital Leadership: Changing paradigms for changing times. Thousand Oaks, CA: Corwin Press.

Schunk, D. H. (1990). Goal setting and self-efficacy during self-regulated learning. Educational Psychologist, 25, 71-86.

Schunk, D. H. (2005). Self-regulated learning: The educational legacy of Paul R. Pintrich. Educational Psychologist, 40, 85-94.

Serravallo, J. (2017). The Writing Strategies Book: Your Everything to Developing

Skilled Writers. Portsmouth, NH: Heinemann.

Shulman, L. (1987). Knowledge and teaching: Foundations of the new reform. Harvard Educational Review, 57, 1-22.

Siemens, G. (2005). Connectivism: Learning theory for the digital age. International Journal of Instructional Technology and Distance Learning, 2(1), January 2005.

Sjøberg, S. (2010). Constructivism and Learning. *International Encyclopedia of Education*. 5: 485-490.

Stephens, D., Cox, R., Downs, A. Goforth, J., Jaeger, L. Matheny, A., Plyler, K., Ray, S., Riser, L., Sawyer, B., Thompson, T., Vickio, K. & Wilcox, C. (2012). I know there ain't no pigs with wigs. Challenges of Tier 2 intervention. *Reading Teacher*, 66(2). 93-103.

Taber, K. (2006). Beyond constructivism: The progressive research programme into learning science. *Studies in Science Education*. 42: 125–184.

Tomlinson, C. (2001): How to differentiate instruction in mixed-ability classrooms. 2nd edition. Alexandria, VA: ASCD.

Toth, S., Evans, R., O'Neal, M., and Highfill, M. (2018). Addressing school district readiness for elementary health education using the transtheoretical model. *Journal of Health Education Teaching*. 9(1): 68-80.

Trowler, V. (2010). Student engagement literature review. *The Higher Education Academy*. Retrieved on November 24, 2020 from https://www.researchgate.net/ publication/322342119_Student_Engagement_Literature_Review

Unicheck. (2015). Digital immigrants vs digital natives: Closing the gap. Retrieved from https:// unicheck.com/blog/digital-immigrants-vs-digital-natives

U.S. Department of Education, Office of Planning, Evaluation and Policy Development (2011). Teachers' Ability to Use Data to Inform Instruction: Challenges and Supports, Washington, D.C.

Vega, V., & Robb, M. B. (2019). The common sense census: Digital Citizenship. San Francisco, CA: Common Sense Media.

Villegas, A. & Lucas, T. (2002). Educating culturally responsive teachers: A coherent approach. Albany: State University of New York Press.

Von Glaserfeld, E. (1995). Radical constructivism: A way of knowing and learning. Washington, D.C.: The Falmer Press.

Ward, B. (1987). Instructional Grouping in the Classroom. *School Improvement Research Series*. Retrieved from https://educationnorthwest.org/sites/default/files/ InstructionalGrouping.pdf.

Whipp, J. L., and Chiarelli, S. (2001). Proposal: Self-regulation in web-based courses for teachers. *Educational Technology Research and Development,* 52(4): 5-21.

Williams, J. B.& Jacobs, J. S. (2004). Exploring the use of blogs as learning spaces in the higher education sector. Australasian journal of educational technology, 20(2), 232-247.

Wilson Smith, S. (2008). *E-Learning.* Vol 5(2). Retrieved on October 14, 2020 from https://journals.sagepub.com/doi/pdf/10.2304/elea.2008.5.2.180.

Wolf, M. (2007). Proust and the squid. The story and science of the reading brain. New York: HarperCollins.

Yoon, K. S., Duncan, T., Lee, S. W.-Y., Scarloss, B., & Shapley, K. (2007). Reviewing the evidence on how teacher professional development affects student achievement (Issues & Answers Report, REL 2007–No. 033). Washington, DC: U.S. Department of Education, Institute of Education Sciences, National Center for Education Evaluation and Regional Assistance, Regional Educational Laboratory Southwest. Retrieved from http://ies.ed.gov/ncee/edlabs.

Yopp, R. H., & Yopp, H. K. (2007). Ten important words plus: a strategy for building word knowledge. *The Reading Teacher, 61(2),* 157-161.

Young, A. & Fulwiler, T. (1986). Writing across the disciplines. Upper Montclair, N.J.: Boynton/Cook.

Young, E. (2010). Challenges to conceptualizing and actualizing culturally relevant pedagogy: How viable is the theory in classroom practice? *Journal of Teacher Education.* 61(3): 248-260.

Zimmerman, B. J. (1998). Developing self-fulfilling cycles of academic regulation: an analysis of exemplary instructional models. In D. H. Schunk and B. J. Zimmerman (Eds.) Self-Regulated Learning: From teaching to self-reflective practice (p. 1-19). New York: The Guilford Press.

Zimmerman, B. J. (1994). Dimensions of academic self-regulation: a conceptual framework for education. In D. H. Schunk and B. J. Zimmerman (Eds.) Self-regulation of learning and performance (p. 3-21). Hillsdale, NJ.: Lawrence Erlbaum Associates.

Zimmerman, B. J. (1989). A social cognitive view of self-regulated academic learning. Journal of Educational Psychology 81(3), 329 – 339.

About the Author

Jami Fowler-White is the CEO of *Digital PD 4 You, LLC*. Over the past two decades, she has served in many capacities in education which include ten years as a classroom teacher, an Instructional Coach, and a Core Advocate with *Achieve the Core*. She currently mentors First-time and Renewal candidates for the National Board, and is a charter member of the National Board Network of Minoritized Educators. Additionally, Mrs. Fowler-White is also a proud member of Delta Sigma Theta Sorority and currently serves as an assistant principal in Shelby County Schools (TN).

Fowler-White also provides professional development under the umbrella of the National Board and *Digital PD 4 You* for schools and districts. She is the author/coauthor of several books including, *Educator Reflection Tips, Volume #1* and *The Skin You are In: Colorism in the Black Community, 2nd Edition*.

Jami blogs at *DigitalPD4You.com*, has a bi-monthly leadership blog on *Insight Advance*, and writes a monthly blog entitled the *Better Mindset* on TeachBetter.com She can be contacted via email at: jwhite.nbct2008@gmail.com and invites you to connect with her on Twitter via @JjJj821

More from ConnectEDD Publishing

S ince 2015, ConnectEDD has worked to transform education by empowering educators to become better-equipped to teach, learn, and lead. What started as a small company designed to provide professional learning events for educators has grown to include a variety of services to help teachers and administrators address essential challenges. ConnectEDD offers instructional and leadership coaching, professional development workshops focusing on a variety of educational topics, a roster of nationally recognized educator associates who possess hands-on knowledge and experience, educational conferences custom-designed to meet the specific needs of schools, districts, and state/national organizations, and ongoing, personalized support, both virtually and onsite. In 2020, ConnectEDD expanded to include publishing services designed to provide busy educators with books and resources consisting of practical information on a wide variety of teaching, learning, and leadership topics. Please visit us online at *connecteddpublishing.com* or contact us at: *info@connecteddpublishing.com*

Recent Publications:

- *Live Your Excellence: Action Guide* by Jimmy Casas
- *Culturize: Action Guide* by Jimmy Casas
- *Daily Inspiration for Educators: Positive Thoughts for Every Day of the Year* by Jimmy Casas
- *Eyes on Culture: Multiply Excellence in Your School* by Emily Paschall
- *Pause. Breathe. Flourish.: Living Your Best Life as an Educator* by William D. Parker
- *L.E.A.R.N.E.R. - Finding the True, Good, and Beautiful in Education* by Marita Diffenbaugh